**EXCELSIOR/REGENTS COLLEGE
EXAMINATIONS**

THIS IS YOUR **PASSBOOK**® FOR ...

PHYSICAL GEOLOGY

NATIONAL LEARNING CORPORATION®
passbooks.com

PASSBOOK® SERIES

THE *PASSBOOK® SERIES* has been created to prepare applicants and candidates for the ultimate academic battlefield – the examination room.

At some time in our lives, each and every one of us may be required to take an examination – for validation, matriculation, admission, qualification, registration, certification, or licensure.

Based on the assumption that every applicant or candidate has met the basic formal educational standards, has taken the required number of courses, and read the necessary texts, the *PASSBOOK® SERIES* furnishes the one special preparation which may assure passing with confidence, instead of failing with insecurity. Examination questions – together with answers – are furnished as the basic vehicle for study so that the mysteries of the examination and its compounding difficulties may be eliminated or diminished by a sure method.

This book is meant to help you pass your examination provided that you qualify and are serious in your objective.

The entire field is reviewed through the huge store of content information which is succinctly presented through a provocative and challenging approach – the question-and-answer method.

A climate of success is established by furnishing the correct answers at the end of each test.

You soon learn to recognize types of questions, forms of questions, and patterns of questioning. You may even begin to anticipate expected outcomes.

You perceive that many questions are repeated or adapted so that you can gain acute insights, which may enable you to score many sure points.

You learn how to confront new questions, or types of questions, and to attack them confidently and work out the correct answers.

You note objectives and emphases, and recognize pitfalls and dangers, so that you may make positive educational adjustments.

Moreover, you are kept fully informed in relation to new concepts, methods, practices, and directions in the field.

You discover that you arre actually taking the examination all the time: you are preparing for the examination by "taking" an examination, not by reading extraneous and/or supererogatory textbooks.

In short, this PASSBOOK®, used directedly, should be an important factor in helping you to pass your test.

NONTRADITIONAL EDUCATION

Students returning to school as adults bring more varied experience to their studies than do the teenagers who begin college shortly after graduating from high school. As a result, there are numerous programs for students with nontraditional learning curves. Hundreds of colleges and universities grant degrees to people who cannot attend classes at a regular campus or have already learned what the college is supposed to teach.

You can earn nontraditional education credits in many ways:

- Passing standardized exams
- Demonstrating knowledge gained through experience
- Completing campus-based coursework, and
- Taking courses off campus

Some methods of assessing learning for credit are objective, such as standardized tests. Others are more subjective, such as a review of life experiences.

With some help from four hypothetical characters – Alice, Vin, Lynette, and Jorge – this article describes nontraditional ways of earning educational credit. It begins by describing programs in which you can earn a high school diploma without spending 4 years in a classroom. The college picture is more complicated, so it is presented in two parts: one on gaining credit for what you know through course work or experience, and a second on college degree programs. The final section lists resources for locating more information.

Earning High School Credit

People who were prevented from finishing high school as teenagers have several options if they want to do so as adults. Some major cities have back-to-school programs that allow adults to attend high school classes with current students. But the more practical alternatives for most adults are to take the General Educational Development (GED) tests or to earn a high school diploma by demonstrating their skills or taking correspondence classes.

Of course, these options do not match the experience of staying in high school and graduating with one's friends. But they are viable alternatives for adult learners committed to meeting and, often, continuing their educational goals.

GED Program

Alice quit high school her sophomore year and took a job to help support herself, her younger brother, and their newly widowed mother. Now an adult, she wants to earn her high school diploma – and then go on to college. Because her job as head cook and her family responsibilities keep her busy during the day, she plans to get a high school equivalency diploma. She will study for, and take, the GED tests. Every year, about half a million adults earn their high school credentials this way. A GED diploma is accepted in lieu of a high school one by more than 90 percent of employers, colleges, and universities, so it is a good choice for someone like Alice.

The GED testing program is sponsored by the American Council on Education and State and local education departments. It consists of examinations in five subject areas: Writing, science, mathematics, social studies, and literature and the arts. The tests also measure skills such as analytical ability, problem solving, reading comprehension, and ability to understand and apply information. Most of the questions are multiple choice; the writing test includes an essay section on a topic of general interest.

Eligibility rules for taking the exams vary, but some states require that you must be at least 18. Tests are given in English, Spanish, and French. In addition to standard print, versions in large print, Braille, and audiocassette are also available. Total time allotted for the tests is 7 1/2 hours.

The GED tests are not easy. About one-fourth of those who complete the exams every year do not pass. Passing scores are established by administering the tests to a sample of graduating high school seniors. The minimum standard score is set so that about one-third of graduating seniors would not pass the tests if they took them.

Because of the difficulty of the tests, people need to prepare themselves to take them. Often, they start by taking the Official GED Practice Tests, usually available through a local adult education center. Centers are listed in your phone book's blue pages under "Adult Education," "Continuing Education," or "GED." Adult education centers also have information about GED preparation classes and self-study materials. Classes are generally arranged to accommodate adults' work schedules. National Learning Corporation publishes several study guides that aim to thoroughly prepare test-takers for the GED.

School districts, colleges, adult education centers, and community organizations have information about GED testing schedules and practice tests. For more information, contact them, your nearest GED testing center, or:

GED Testing Service
One Dupont Circle, NW, Suite 250
Washington, DC 20036-1163
1(800) 62-MY GED (626-9433)
(202) 939-9490

Skills Demonstration

Adults who have acquired high school level skills through experience might be eligible for the National External Diploma Program. This alternative to the GED does not involve any direct instruction. Instead, adults seeking a high school diploma must demonstrate mastery of 65 competencies in 8 general areas: Communication; computation; occupational preparedness; and self, social, consumer, scientific, and technological awareness.

Mastery is shown through the completion of the tasks. For example, a participant could prove competency in computation by measuring a room for carpeting, figuring out the amount of carpet needed, and computing the cost.

Before being accepted for the program, adults undergo an evaluation. Tests taken at one of the program's offices measure reading, writing, and mathematics abilities. A take-home segment includes a self-assessment of current skills, an individual skill evaluation, and an occupational interest and aptitude test.

Adults accepted for the program have weekly meetings with an assessor. At the meeting, the assessor reviews the participant's work from the previous week. If the task has not been completed properly, the assessor explains the mistake. Participants continue to correct their errors until they master each competency. A high school diploma is awarded upon proven mastery of all 65 competencies.

Fourteen States and the District of Columbia now offer the External Diploma Program. For more information, contact:

External Diploma Program
One Dupont Circle, NW, Suite 250
Washington, DC 20036-1193
(202) 939-9475

Correspondence and Distance Study

Vin dropped out of high school during his junior year because his family's frequent moves made it difficult for him to continue his studies. He promised himself at the time he dropped out that he would someday finish the courses needed for his diploma. For people like Vin, who prefer to earn a traditional diploma in a nontraditional way, there are about a dozen accredited courses of study for earning a high school diploma by correspondence, or distance study. The programs are either privately run, affiliated with a university, or administered by a State education department.

Distance study diploma programs have no residency requirements, allowing students to continue their studies from almost any location. Depending on the course of study, students need not be enrolled full time and usually have more flexible schedules for finishing their work. Selection of courses ranges from vo-tech to college prep, and some programs place different emphasis on the types of diplomas offered. University affiliated schools, for example, allow qualified students to take college courses along with their high school ones. Students can then apply the college credits toward a degree at that university or transfer them to another institution.

Taking courses by distance study is often more challenging and time consuming than attending classes, especially for adults who have other obligations. Success depends on each student's motivation. Students usually do reading assignments on their own. Written exercises, which they complete and send to an instructor for grading, supplement their reading material.

A list of some accredited high schools that offer diplomas by distance study is available free from the Distance Education and Training Council, formerly known as the National Home Study Council. Request the "DETC Directory of Accredited Institutions" from:

The Distance Education and Training Council
1601 18th Street, NW.
Washington, DC 20009-2529
(202) 234-5100

Some publications profiling nontraditional college programs include addresses and descriptions of several high school correspondence ones. See the Resources section at the end of this article for more information.

Getting College Credit For What You Know

Adults can receive college credit for prior coursework, by passing examinations, and documenting experiential learning. With help from a college advisor, nontraditional students should assess their skills, establish their educational goals, and determine the number of college credits they might be eligible for.

Even before you meet with a college advisor, you should collect all your school and training records. Then, make a list of all knowledge and abilities acquired through experience, no matter how irrelevant they seem to your chosen field. Next, determine your educational goals: What specific field do you wish to study? What kind of a degree do you want? Finally, determine how your past work fits into the field of study. Later on, you will evaluate educational programs to find one that's right for you.

People who have complex educational or experiential learning histories might want to have their learning evaluated by the Regents Credit Bank. The Credit Bank, operated by Regents College of the University of the State of New York, allows people to consolidate credits earned through college, experience, or other methods. Special assessments are available for Regents College enrollees whose knowledge in a specific field cannot be adequately evaluated by standardized exams. For more information, contact the Regents Credit Bank at:

Regents College
7 Columbia Circle
Albany, NY 12203-5159
(518) 464-8500

Credit For Prior College Coursework

When Lynette was in college during the 1970s, she attended several different schools and took a variety of courses. She did well in some classes and poorly in others. Now that she is a successful business owner and has more focus, Lynette thinks she should forget about her previous coursework and start from scratch. Instead, she should start from where she is.

Lynette should have all her transcripts sent to the colleges or universities of her choice and let an admissions officer determine which classes are applicable toward a degree. A few credits here and there may not seem like much, but they add up. Even if the subjects do not seem relevant to any major, they might be counted as elective credits toward a degree. And comparing the cost of transcripts with the cost of college courses, it makes sense to spend a few dollars per transcript for a chance to save hundreds, and perhaps thousands, of dollars in books and tuition.

Rules for transferring credits apply to all prior coursework at accredited colleges and universities, whether done on campus or off. Courses completed off campus, often called extended learning, include those available to students through independent study and correspondence. Many schools have extended learning programs; Brigham Young University, for example, offers more than 300 courses through its Department of Independent Study. One type of extended learning is distance learning, a form of correspondence study by technological means such as television, video and audio, CD-ROM, electronic mail, and computer tutorials. See the Resources section at the end of this article for more information about publications available from the National University Continuing Education Association.

Any previously earned college credits should be considered for transfer, no matter what the subject or the grade received. Many schools do not accept the transfer of courses graded below a C or ones taken more than a designated number of years ago. Some colleges and universities also have limits on the number of credits that can be transferred and applied toward a degree. But not all do. For example, Thomas Edison State College, New Jersey's State college for adults, accepts the transfer of all 120 hours of credit required for a baccalaureate degree – provided all the credits are transferred from regionally accredited schools, no more than 80 are at the junior college level, and the student's grades overall and in the field of study average out to C.

To assign credit for prior coursework, most schools require original transcripts. This means you must complete a form or send a written, signed request to have your transcripts released directly to a college or university. Once you have chosen the schools you want to apply to, contact the schools you attended before. Find out how much each transcript costs, and ask them to send your transcripts to the ones you are applying to. Write a letter that includes your name (and names used during attendance, if different) and dates of attendance, along with the names and addresses of the schools to which your transcripts should be sent. Include payment and mail to the registrar at the schools you have attended. The registrar's office will process your request and send an official transcript of your coursework to the colleges or universities you have designated.

Credit For Noncollege Courses

Colleges and universities are not the only ones that offer classes. Volunteer organizations and employers often provide formal training worth college credit. The American Council on Education has two programs that assess thousands of specific courses and make recommendations on the amount of college credit they are worth. Colleges and universities accept the recommendations or use them as guidelines.

One program evaluates educational courses sponsored by government agencies, business and industry, labor unions, and professional and voluntary organizations. It is the Program on Noncollegiate Sponsored Instruction (PONSI). Some of the training seminars Alice has participated in covered topics such as food preparation, kitchen safety, and nutrition. Although she has not yet earned her GED, Alice can earn college credit because of her completion of these formal job-training seminars. The number of credits each seminar is worth does not hinge on Alice's current eligibility for college enrollment.

The other program evaluates courses offered by the Army, Navy, Air Force, Marines, Coast Guard, and Department of Defense. It is the Military Evaluations Program. Jorge has never attended college, but the engineering technology classes he completed as part of his military training are worth college credit. And as an Army veteran, Jorge is eligible for a service that takes the evaluations one step further. The Army/American Council on Education Registry Transcript System (AARTS) will provide Jorge with an individualized transcript of American Council on Education credit recommendations for all courses he completed, the military occupational specialties (MOS's) he held, and examinations he passed while in the Army. All Army and National Guard enlisted personnel and veterans who enlisted after October 1981 are eligible for the transcript. Similar services are being considered by the Navy and Marine Corps.

To obtain a free transcript, see your Army Education Center for a 5454R transcript request form. Include your name, Social Security number, basic active service date, and complete address where you want the transcript sent. Mail your request to:

AARTS Operations Center
415 McPherson Ave.
Fort Leavenworth, KS 66027-1373

Recommendations for PONSI are published in *The National Guide to Educational Credit for Training Programs;* military program recommendations are in *The Guide to the Evaluation of Educational Experiences in the Armed Forces.* See the Resources section at the end of this article for more information about these publications.

Former military personnel who took a foreign language course through the Defense Language Institute may request course transcripts by sending their name, Social Security number, course title, duration of the course, and graduation date to:

Commandant, Defense Language Institute
Attn: ATFL-DAA-AR
Transcripts
Presidio of Monterey
Monterey, CA 93944-5006

Not all of Jorge's and Alice's courses have been assessed by the American Council on Education. Training courses that have no Council credit recommendation should still be assessed by an advisor at the schools they want to attend. Course descriptions, class notes, test scores, and other documentation may be helpful for comparing training courses to their college equivalents. An oral examination or other demonstration of competency might also be required.

There is no guarantee you will receive all the credits you are seeking – but you certainly won't if you make no attempt.

Credit By Examination

Standardized tests are the best-known method of receiving college credit without taking courses. These exams are often taken by high school students seeking advanced placement for college, but they are also available to adult learners. Testing programs and colleges and universities offer exams in a number of subjects. Two U.S. Government institutes have foreign language exams for employees that also may be worth college credit.

It is important to understand that receiving a passing score on these exams does not mean you get college credit automatically. Each school determines which test results it will accept, minimum scores required, how scores are converted for credit, and the amount of credit, if any, to be assigned. Most colleges and universities accept the American Council on Education credit recommendations, published every other year in the 250-page *Guide to Educational Credit by Examination*. For more information, contact:

The American Council on Education
Credit by Examination Program
One Dupont Circle, Suite 250
Washington, DC 20036-1193
(202) 939-9434

Testing programs:

You might know some of the five national testing programs by their acronyms or initials: CLEP, ACT PEP: RCE, DANTES, AP, and NOCTI. (The meanings of these initialisms are explained below.) There is some overlap among programs; for example, four of them have introductory accounting exams. Since you will not be awarded credit more than once for a specific subject, you should carefully evaluate each program for the subject exams you wish to take. And before taking an exam, make sure you will be awarded credit by the college or university you plan to attend.

CLEP (College-Level Examination Program), administered by the College Board, is the most widely accepted of the national testing programs; more than 2,800 accredited schools award credit for passing exam scores. Each test covers material taught in basic undergraduate courses. There are five general exams – English composition, humanities, college mathematics, natural sciences, and social sciences and history – and many subject exams. Most exams are entirely multiple-choice, but English composition exams may include an essay section. For more information, contact:

CLEP
P.O. Box 6600
Princeton, NJ 08541-6600
(609) 771-7865

ACT PEP: RCE (American College Testing Proficiency Exam Program: Regents College Examinations) tests are given in 38 subjects within arts and sciences, business, education, and nursing. Each exam is recommended for either lower- or upper-level credit. Exams contain either objective or extended response questions, and are graded according to a standard score, letter grade, or pass/fail. Fees vary, depending on the subject and type of exam. For more information or to request free study guides, contact:

ACT PEP: Regents College Examinations
P.O. Box 4014
Iowa City, IA 52243
(319) 337-1387
(New York State residents must contact Regents College directly.)

DANTES (Defense Activity for Nontraditional Education Support) standardized tests are developed by the Educational Testing Service for the Department of Defense. Originally administered only to military personnel, the exams have been available to the public since 1983. About 50 subject tests cover business, mathematics, social science, physical science, humanities, foreign languages, and applied technology. Most of the tests consist entirely of multiple-choice questions. Schools determine their own administering fees and testing schedules. For more information or to request free study sheets, contact:

DANTES Program Office
Mail Stop 31-X
Educational Testing Service
Princeton, NJ 08541
1(800) 257-9484

The AP (Advanced Placement) Program is a cooperative effort between secondary schools and colleges and universities. AP exams are developed each year by committees of college and high school faculty appointed by the College Board and assisted by consultants from the Educational Testing Service. Subjects include arts and languages, natural sciences, computer science, social sciences, history, and mathematics. Most tests are 2 or 3 hours long and include both multiple-choice and essay questions. AP courses are available to help students prepare for exams, which are offered in the spring. For more information about the Advanced Placement Program, contact:

Advanced Placement Services
P.O. Box 6671
Princeton, NJ 08541-6671
(609) 771-7300

NOCTI (National Occupational Competency Testing Institute) assessments are designed for people like Alice, who have vocational-technical skills that cannot be evaluated by other tests. NOCTI assesses competency at two levels: Student/job ready and teacher/experienced worker. Standardized evaluations are available for occupations such as auto-body repair, electronics, mechanical drafting, quantity food preparation, and upholstering. The tests consist of multiple-choice questions and a performance component. Other services include workshops, customized assessments, and pre-testing. For more information, contact:

NOCTI
500 N. Bronson Ave.
Ferris State University
Big Rapids, MI 49307
(616) 796-4699

Colleges and universities:

Many colleges and universities have credit-by-exam programs, through which students earn credit by passing a comprehensive exam for a course offered by the institution. Among the most widely recognized are the programs at Ohio University, the University of North Carolina, Thomas Edison State College, and New York University.

Ohio University offers about 150 examinations for credit. In addition, you may sometimes arrange to take special examinations in non-laboratory courses offered at Ohio University. To take a test for credit, you must enroll in the course. If you plan to transfer the credit earned, you also need written permission from an official at your school. Books and study materials are available, for a cost, through the university. Exams must be taken within 6 months of the enrollment date; most last 3 hours. You may arrange to take the exam off campus if you do not live near the university.

Ohio University is on the quarter-hour system; most courses are worth 4 quarter hours, the equivalent of 3 semester hours. For more information, contact:

Independent Study
Tupper Hall 302
Ohio University
Athens, OH 45701-2979
1(800) 444-2910
(614) 593-2910

The University of North Carolina offers a credit-by-examination option for 140 independent study (correspondence) courses in foreign languages, humanities, social sciences, mathematics, business administration, education, electrical and computer engineering, health administration, and natural sciences. To take an exam, you must request and receive approval from both the course instructor and the independent studies department. Exams must be taken within six months of enrollment, and you may register for no more than two at a time. If you are not near the University's Chapel Hill campus, you may take your exam under supervision at an accredited college, university, community college, or technical institute. For more information, contact:

Independent Studies
CB #1020, The Friday Center
UNC-Chapel Hill
Chapel Hill, NC 27599-1020
1(800) 862-5669 / (919) 962-1134

The Thomas Edison College Examination Program offers more than 50 exams in liberal arts, business, and professional areas. Thomas Edison State College administers tests twice a month in Trenton, New Jersey; however, students may arrange to take their tests with a proctor at any accredited American college or university or U.S. military base. Most of the tests are multiple choice; some also include short answer or essay questions. Time limits range from 90 minutes to 4 hours, depending on the exam. For more information, contact:

Thomas Edison State College
TECEP, Office of Testing and Assessment
101 W. State Street
Trenton, NJ 08608-1176
(609) 633-2844

New York University's Foreign Language Program offers proficiency exams in more than 40 languages, from Albanian to Yiddish. Two exams are available in each language: The 12-point test is equivalent to 4 undergraduate semesters, and the 16-point exam may lead to upper level credit. The tests are given at the university's Foreign Language Department throughout the year.

Proof of foreign language proficiency does not guarantee college credit. Some colleges and universities accept transcripts only for languages commonly taught, such as French and Spanish. Nontraditional programs are more likely than traditional ones to grant credit for proficiency in other languages.

For an informational brochure and registration form for NYU's foreign language proficiency exams, contact:

New York University
Foreign Language Department
48 Cooper Square, Room 107
New York, NY 10003
(212) 998-7030

Government institutes:

The Defense Language Institute and Foreign Service Institute administer foreign language proficiency exams for personnel stationed abroad. Usually, the tests are given at the end of intensive language courses or upon completion of service overseas. But some people – like Jorge, who knows Spanish – speak another language fluently and may be allowed to take a proficiency exam in that language before completing their tour of duty. Contact one of the offices listed below to obtain transcripts of those scores. Proof of proficiency does not guarantee college credit, however, as discussed above.

To request score reports from the Defense Language Institute for Defense Language Proficiency Tests, send your name, Social Security number, language for which you were tested, and, most importantly, when and where you took the exam to:

Commandant, Defense Language Institute
Attn: ATFL-ES-T
DLPT Score Report Request
Presidio of Monterey
Monterey, CA 93944-5006

To request transcripts of scores for Foreign Service Institute exams, send your name, Social Security number, language for which you were tested, and dates or year of exams to:

Foreign Service Institute
Arlington Hall
4020 Arlington Boulevard
Rosslyn, VA 22204-1500
Attn: Testing Office (Send your request to the attention of the testing office of the foreign language in which you were tested)

Credit For Experience

Experiential learning credit may be given for knowledge gained through job responsibilities, personal hobbies, volunteer opportunities, homemaking, and other experiences. Colleges and universities base credit awards on the knowledge you have attained, not for the experience alone. In addition, the knowledge must be college level; not just any learning will do. Throwing horseshoes as a hobby is not likely to be worth college credit. But if you've done research on how and where the sport originated, visited blacksmiths, organized tournaments, and written a column for a trade journal — well, that's a horseshoe of a different color.

Adults attempting to get credit for their experience should be forewarned: Having your experience evaluated for college credit is time-consuming, tedious work – not an easy shortcut for people who want quick-fix college credits. And not all experience, no matter how valuable, is the equivalent of college courses.

Requesting college credit for your experiential learning can be tricky. You should get assistance from a credit evaluations officer at the school you plan to attend, but you should also have a general idea of what your knowledge is worth. A common method for converting knowledge into credit is to use a college catalog. Find course titles and descriptions that match what you have learned through experience, and request the number of credits offered for those courses.

Once you know what credit to ask for, you must usually present your case in writing to officials at the college you plan to attend. The most common form of presenting experiential learning for credit is the portfolio. A portfolio is a written record of your knowledge along with a request for equivalent college credit. It includes an identification and description of the knowledge for which you are requesting credit, an explanatory essay of how the knowledge was gained and how it fits into your educational plans, documentation that you have acquired such knowledge, and a request for college credit. Required elements of a portfolio vary by schools but generally follow those guidelines.

In identifying knowledge you have gained, be specific about exactly what you have learned. For example, it is not enough for Lynette to say she runs a business. She must identify the knowledge she has gained from running it, such as personnel management, tax law, marketing strategy, and inventory review. She must also include brief descriptions about her knowledge of each to support her claims of having those skills.

The essay gives you a chance to relay something about who you are. It should address your educational goals, include relevant autobiographical details, and be well organized, neat, and convey confidence. In his essay, Jorge might first state his goal of becoming an engineer. Then he would explain why he joined the Army, where he got hands-on training and experience in developing and servicing electronic equipment.

This, he would say, led to his hobby of creating remote-controlled model cars, of which he has built 20. His conclusion would highlight his accomplishments and tie them to his desire to become an electronic engineer.

Documentation is evidence that you've learned what you claim to have learned. You can show proof of knowledge in a variety of ways, including audio or video recordings, letters from current or former employers describing your specific duties and job performance, blueprints, photographs or artwork, and transcripts of certifying exams for professional licenses and certification – such as Alice's certification from the American Culinary Federation. Although documentation can take many forms, written proof alone is not always enough. If it is impossible to document your knowledge in writing, find out if your experiential learning can be assessed through supplemental oral exams by a faculty expert.

Earning a College Degree

Nontraditional students often have work, family, and financial obligations that prevent them from quitting their jobs to attend school full time. Can they still meet their educational goals? Yes.

More than 150 accredited colleges and universities have nontraditional bachelor's degree programs that require students to spend little or no time on campus; over 300 others have nontraditional campus-based degree programs. Some of those schools, as well as most junior and community colleges, offer associate's degrees nontraditionally. Each school with a nontraditional course of study determines its own rules for awarding credit for prior coursework, exams, or experience, as discussed previously. Most have charges on top of tuition for providing these special services.

Several publications profile nontraditional degree programs; see the Resources section at the end of this article for more information. To determine which school best fits your academic profile and educational goals, first list your criteria. Then, evaluate nontraditional programs based on their accreditation, features, residency requirements, and expenses. Once you have chosen several schools to explore further, write to them for more information. Detailed explanations of school policies should help you decide which ones you want to apply to.

Get beyond the printed word – especially the glowing words each school writes about itself. Check out the schools you are considering with higher education authorities, alumni, employers, family members, and friends. If possible, visit the campus to talk to students and instructors and sit in on a few classes, even if you will be completing most or all of your work off campus. Ask school officials questions about such things as enrollment numbers, graduation rate, faculty qualifications, and confusing details about the application process or academic policies. After you have thoroughly investigated each prospective college or university, you can make an informed decision about which is right for you.

Accreditation

Accreditation is a process colleges and universities submit to voluntarily for getting their credentials. An accredited school has been investigated and visited by teams of observers and has periodic inspections by a private accrediting agency. The initial review can take two years or more.

Regional agencies accredit entire schools, and professional agencies accredit either specialized schools or departments within schools. Although there are no national accrediting standards, not just any accreditation will do. Countless "accreditation associations" have been invented by schools, many of which have no academic programs and sell phony degrees, to accredit themselves. But 6 regional and about 80 professional accrediting associations in the United States are recognized by the U.S. Department of Education or the Commission on Recognition of Postsecondary Accreditation. When checking accreditation, these are the names to look for. For more information about accreditation and accrediting agencies, contact:

Institutional Participation Oversight Service Accreditation and State Liaison Division
U.S. Department of Education
ROB 3, Room 3915
600 Independence Ave., SW
Washington, DC 20202-5244
(202) 708-7417

Because accreditation is not mandatory, lack of accreditation does not necessarily mean a school or program is bad. Some schools choose not to apply for accreditation, are in the process of applying, or have educational methods too unconventional for an accrediting association's standards. For the nontraditional student, however, earning a degree from a college or university with recognized accreditation is an especially important consideration. Although nontraditional education is becoming more widely accepted, it is not yet mainstream. Employers skeptical of a degree earned in a nontraditional manner are likely to be even less accepting of one from an unaccredited school.

Program Features

Because nontraditional students have diverse educational objectives, nontraditional schools are diverse in what they offer. Some programs are geared toward helping students organize their scattered educational credits to get a degree as quickly as possible. Others cater to those who may have specific credits or experience but need assistance in completing requirements. Whatever your educational profile, you should look for a program that works with you in obtaining your educational goals.

A few nontraditional programs have special admissions policies for adult learners like Alice, who plan to earn their GEDs but want to enroll in college in the meantime. Other features of nontraditional programs include individualized learning agreements, intensive academic counseling, cooperative learning and internship placement, and waiver of some prerequisites or other requirements – as well as college credit for prior coursework, examinations, and experiential learning, all discussed previously.

Lynette, whose primary goal is to finish her degree, wants to earn maximum credits for her business experience. She will look for programs that do not limit the number of credits awarded for equivalency exams and experiential learning. And since well-documented proof of knowledge is essential for earning experiential learning credits, Lynette should make sure the program she chooses provides assistance to students submitting a portfolio.

Jorge, on the other hand, has more credits than he needs in certain areas and is willing to forego some. To become an engineer, he must have a bachelor's degree; but because he is accustomed to hands-on learning, Jorge is interested in getting experience as he gains more technical skills. He will concentrate on finding schools with strong cooperative education, supervised fieldwork, or internship programs.

Residency Requirements

Programs are sometimes deemed nontraditional because of their residency requirements. Many people think of residency for colleges and universities in terms of tuition, with in-state students paying less than out-of-state ones. Residency also may refer to where a student lives, either on or off campus, while attending school.

But in nontraditional education, residency usually refers to how much time students must spend on campus, regardless of whether they attend classes there. In some nontraditional programs, students need not ever step foot on campus. Others require only a very short residency, such as one day or a few weeks. Many schools have standard residency requirements of several semesters but schedule classes for evenings or weekends to accommodate working adults.

Lynette, who previously took courses by independent study, prefers to earn credits by distance study. She will focus on schools that have no residency requirement. Several colleges and universities have nonresident degree completion programs for adults with some college credit. Under the direction of a faculty advisor, students devise a plan for earning their remaining credits. Methods for earning credits include independent study, distance learning, seminars, supervised fieldwork, and group study at arranged sites. Students may have to earn a certain number of credits through the degree-granting institution. But many programs allow students to take courses at accredited schools of their choice for transfer toward their degree.

Alice wants to attend lectures but has an unpredictable schedule. Her best course of action will be to seek out short residency programs that require students to attend seminars once or twice a semester. She can take courses that are televised and videotape them to watch when her schedule permits, with the seminars helping to ensure that she properly completes her coursework. Many colleges and universities with short residency requirements also permit students to earn some credits elsewhere, by whatever means the student chooses.

Some fields of study require classroom instruction. As Jorge will discover, few colleges and universities allow students to earn a bachelor's degree in engineering entirely through independent study. Nontraditional residency programs are designed to accommodate adults' daytime work schedules. Jorge should look for programs offering evening, weekend, summer, and accelerated courses.

Tuition and Other Expenses

The final decisions about which schools Alice, Jorge, and Lynette attend may hinge in large part on a single issue: Cost. And rising tuition is only part of the equation. Beginning with application fees and continuing through graduation fees, college expenses add up.

Traditional and nontraditional students have some expenses in common, such as the cost of books and other materials. Tuition might even be the same for some courses, especially for colleges and universities offering standard ones at unusual times. But for nontraditional programs, students may also pay fees for services such as credit or transcript review, evaluation, advisement, and portfolio assessment.

Students are also responsible for postage and handling or setup expenses for independent study courses, as well as for all examination and transcript fees for transferring credits. Usually, the more nontraditional the program, the more detailed the fees. Some schools charge a yearly enrollment fee rather than tuition for degree completion candidates who want their files to remain active.

Although tuition and fees might seem expensive, most educators tell you not to let money come between you and your educational goals. Talk to someone in the financial aid department of the school you plan to attend or check your library for publications about financial aid sources. The U.S. Department of Education publishes a guide to Federal aid programs such as Pell Grants, student loans, and work-study. To order the free 74-page booklet, *The Student Guide: Financial Aid from the U.S. Department of Education,* contact:

Federal Student Aid Information Center
P.O. Box 84
Washington, DC 20044
1 (800) 4FED-AID (433-3243)

Resources

Information on how to earn a high school diploma or college degree without following the usual routes is available from several organizations and in numerous publications. Information on nontraditional graduate degree programs, available for master's through doctoral level, though not discussed in this article, can usually be obtained from the same resources that detail bachelor's degree programs.

National Learning Corporation publishes study guides for all of these exams, for both general examinations and tests in specific subject areas. To order study guides, or to browse their catalog featuring more than 5,000 titles, visit NLC online at www.passbooks.com, or contact them by phone at (800) 632-8888.

Organizations

Adult learners should always contact their local school system, community college, or university to learn about programs that are readily available. The following national organizations can also supply information:

American Council on Education
One Dupont Circle
Washington, DC 20036-1193
(202) 939-9300

Within the American Council on Education, the Center for Adult Learning and Educational Credentials administers the National External Diploma Program, the GED Program, the Program on Noncollegiate Sponsored Instruction, the Credit by Examination Program, and the Military Evaluations Program.

EXCELSIOR/REGENTS COLLEGE EXAMINATIONS (E/RCE)

With Excelsior/Regents College Examinations, you can show what you know and earn the college-level credit you deserve. If you're like many adults today, you've worked hard to get where you are personally and professionally, and are working even harder to improve your situation. You're looking for a way to earn the college degree you've always wanted, and want your past training and experiences to apply toward that degree. Or perhaps you are interested in pursuing independent study in a subject for which Excelsior/Regents College Examinations offer credit. Either way, when you're ready, you can earn three or more credit hours with each Excelsior/Regents College Examination you take.

You don't have to be enrolled in Excelsior/Regents College to gain credit by examination. Credit earned by taking Excelsior/Regents College Examinations may be used at more than 900 other colleges and universities in the United States.

Excelsior/Regents College offers 32 highly respected degree programs for adult learners in Business, Liberal Arts, Nursing, and Technology. It's difficult for many adults to suspend life's everyday demands to go back to school. That's why the Excelsior/Regents College offers adult learners something unique—the opportunity to complete a degree without attending classes in a traditional college setting.

The Excelsior/Regents College degree programs combine independent study, classwork at colleges and universities throughout the world, coursework accomplished on the job, televised and Internet distance learning classes, and examinations for college credit like Excelsior/Regents College Examinations.

The Excelsior/Regents College specialize in providing adults a variety of ways to demonstrate the knowledge they've gained on the job or through past educational experiences and to earn college-level credit for it.

Excelsior/Regents College Examinations are college-level examinations that are used by more than 900 colleges and universities in the United States to award credit or advanced placement. Excelsior/Regents College Examinations provide flexible opportunities for adults to demonstrate their college-level knowledge in the arts and sciences, business, education, and nursing. They enable colleges to offer students options such as advanced placement and exemption from course requirements, and give employers a means to allow employees to earn credit toward job advancement or to pursue a college education without interrupting work schedules. Excelsior/Regents College Examinations credit has also been used toward teach certification or advancement and in fulfillment of civil service qualifications and continuing education requirements.

Registration

Registration materials for Excelsior/Regents College Examinations can be obtained by a variety of means. Detailed information about the administration of the exams, testing center locations, fees, provisions for international and reasonable accommodations testing, and complete instructions for registering are included in the free registration packet. Request the registration packet as follows:

Postal mail: The Administration
     Regents College
     7 Columbia Circle
     Albany, New York 12203-5159

Telephone: 888-RCEXAMS

Fax: (518) 464-8777

E-mail: testadmin@regents.edu

TDD   (518) 464-8501

Web: www.regents.edu/804.htm

When you're ready to demonstrate what you've learned, you can complete the registration process by the traditional mail method or, for faster eligibility, register entirely by phone. Phone registration is very simple: Call 1-888-RCEXAMS, toll-free, to register using your credit card. Once your registration is complete, you will receive an Authorization to Test letter that will admit you to the Sylvan Technology Center you choose. You will have 90 days to schedule your exam by calling Sylvan directly, toll-free.

Test Development and Scoring

A committee of faculty determined the content to be tested on each Excelsior/Regents College examination. Committee members are teaching faculty and practicing professionals in the field covered by the exam. The Excelsior/Regents College Assessment Unit staff oversee the technical aspects of test construction in accordance with current professional standards.

Multiple-choice examinations may contain anywhere from 80 to 160 four-option multiple-choice questions, some of which are unscored, experimental questions. Extended response and mixed format examinations will have fewer questions that you must answer at some length. Since you will not be able to tell which questions are experimental, you should do your best on all of them. Scores are based on ability level as defined in the item response theory (IRT) method of examination development, rather than simply your total number of correct answers. Your score will be reported as a letter grade.

PHYSICAL GEOLOGY

Tests material typically taught in an introductory, one-semester course in physical geology. The exam measures knowledge and understanding of: the processes which form the earth through geologic time; the structure, composition, and evolution of the earth; and the landforms created by the processes which form the earth.

HOW TO TAKE A TEST

You have studied long, hard and conscientiously.

With your official admission card in hand, and your heart pounding, you have been admitted to the examination room.

You note that there are several hundred other applicants in the examination room waiting to take the same test.

They all appear to be equally well prepared.

You know that nothing but your best effort will suffice. The "moment of truth" is at hand: you now have to demonstrate objectively, in writing, your knowledge of content and your understanding of subject matter.

You are fighting the most important battle of your life—to pass and/or score high on an examination which will determine your career and provide the economic basis for your livelihood.

What extra, special things should you know and should you do in taking the examination?

I. YOU MUST PASS AN EXAMINATION

A. WHAT EVERY CANDIDATE SHOULD KNOW
Examination applicants often ask us for help in preparing for the written test. What can I study in advance? What kinds of questions will be asked? How will the test be given? How will the papers be graded?

B. HOW ARE EXAMS DEVELOPED?
Examinations are carefully written by trained technicians who are specialists in the field known as "psychological measurement," in consultation with recognized authorities in the field of work that the test will cover. These experts recommend the subject matter areas or skills to be tested; only those knowledges or skills important to your success on the job are included. The most reliable books and source materials available are used as references. Together, the experts and technicians judge the difficulty level of the questions.

Test technicians know how to phrase questions so that the problem is clearly stated. Their ethics do not permit "trick" or "catch" questions. Questions may have been tried out on sample groups, or subjected to statistical analysis, to determine their usefulness.

Written tests are often used in combination with performance tests, ratings of training and experience, and oral interviews. All of these measures combine to form the best-known means of finding the right person for the right job.

II. HOW TO PASS THE WRITTEN TEST

A. BASIC STEPS

1) Study the announcement

How, then, can you know what subjects to study? Our best answer is: "Learn as much as possible about the class of positions for which you've applied." The exam will test the knowledge, skills and abilities needed to do the work.

Your most valuable source of information about the position you want is the official exam announcement. This announcement lists the training and experience qualifications. Check these standards and apply only if you come reasonably close to meeting them. Many jurisdictions preview the written test in the exam announcement by including a section called "Knowledge and Abilities Required," "Scope of the Examination," or some similar heading. Here you will find out specifically what fields will be tested.

2) Choose appropriate study materials

If the position for which you are applying is technical or advanced, you will read more advanced, specialized material. If you are already familiar with the basic principles of your field, elementary textbooks would waste your time. Concentrate on advanced textbooks and technical periodicals. Think through the concepts and review difficult problems in your field.

These are all general sources. You can get more ideas on your own initiative, following these leads. For example, training manuals and publications of the government agency which employs workers in your field can be useful, particularly for technical and professional positions. A letter or visit to the government department involved may result in more specific study suggestions, and certainly will provide you with a more definite idea of the exact nature of the position you are seeking.

3) Study this book!

III. KINDS OF TESTS

Tests are used for purposes other than measuring knowledge and ability to perform specified duties. For some positions, it is equally important to test ability to make adjustments to new situations or to profit from training. In others, basic mental abilities not dependent on information are essential. Questions which test these things may not appear as pertinent to the duties of the position as those which test for knowledge and information. Yet they are often highly important parts of a fair examination. For very general questions, it is almost impossible to help you direct your study efforts. What we can do is to point out some of the more common of these general abilities needed in public service positions and describe some typical questions.

1) General information

Broad, general information has been found useful for predicting job success in some kinds of work. This is tested in a variety of ways, from vocabulary lists to questions about current events. Basic background in some field of work, such as sociology or economics, may be sampled in a group of questions. Often these are principles which have become familiar to most persons through exposure rather than through formal training. It is difficult to advise you how to study for these questions; being alert to the world around you is our best suggestion.

2) Verbal ability

An example of an ability needed in many positions is verbal or language ability. Verbal ability is, in brief, the ability to use and understand words. Vocabulary and grammar tests are typical measures of this ability. Reading comprehension or paragraph interpretation questions are common in many kinds of civil service tests. You are given a paragraph of written material and asked to find its central meaning.

IV. KINDS OF QUESTIONS

1. Multiple-choice Questions

Most popular of the short-answer questions is the "multiple choice" or "best answer" question. It can be used, for example, to test for factual knowledge, ability to solve problems or judgment in meeting situations found at work.

A multiple-choice question is normally one of three types:

- It can begin with an incomplete statement followed by several possible endings. You are to find the one ending which *best* completes the statement, although some of the others may not be entirely wrong.
- It can also be a complete statement in the form of a question which is answered by choosing one of the statements listed.
- It can be in the form of a problem – again you select the best answer.

Here is an example of a multiple-choice question with a discussion which should give you some clues as to the method for choosing the right answer:

When an employee has a complaint about his assignment, the action which will *best* help him overcome his difficulty is to
- A. discuss his difficulty with his coworkers
- B. take the problem to the head of the organization
- C. take the problem to the person who gave him the assignment
- D. say nothing to anyone about his complaint

In answering this question, you should study each of the choices to find which is best. Consider choice "A" – Certainly an employee may discuss his complaint with fellow employees, but no change or improvement can result, and the complaint remains unresolved. Choice "B" is a poor choice since the head of the organization probably does not know what assignment you have been given, and taking your problem to him is known as "going over the head" of the supervisor. The supervisor, or person who made the assignment, is the person who can clarify it or correct any injustice. Choice "C" is, therefore, correct. To say nothing, as in choice "D," is unwise. Supervisors have and interest in knowing the problems employees are facing, and the employee is seeking a solution to his problem.

2. True/False

3. Matching Questions

Matching an answer from a column of choices within another column.

V. RECORDING YOUR ANSWERS

Computer terminals are used more and more today for many different kinds of exams.

For an examination with very few applicants, you may be told to record your answers in the test booklet itself. Separate answer sheets are much more common. If this separate answer sheet is to be scored by machine – and this is often the case – it is highly important that you mark your answers correctly in order to get credit.

VI. BEFORE THE TEST

YOUR PHYSICAL CONDITION IS IMPORTANT

If you are not well, you can't do your best work on tests. If you are half asleep, you can't do your best either. Here are some tips:

1) Get about the same amount of sleep you usually get. Don't stay up all night before the test, either partying or worrying—DON'T DO IT!
2) If you wear glasses, be sure to wear them when you go to take the test. This goes for hearing aids, too.
3) If you have any physical problems that may keep you from doing your best, be sure to tell the person giving the test. If you are sick or in poor health, you relay cannot do your best on any test. You can always come back and take the test some other time.

Common sense will help you find procedures to follow to get ready for an examination. Too many of us, however, overlook these sensible measures. Indeed, nervousness and fatigue have been found to be the most serious reasons why applicants fail to do their best on civil service tests. Here is a list of reminders:

- Begin your preparation early – Don't wait until the last minute to go scurrying around for books and materials or to find out what the position is all about.
- Prepare continuously – An hour a night for a week is better than an all-night cram session. This has been definitely established. What is more, a night a week for a month will return better dividends than crowding your study into a shorter period of time.
- Locate the place of the exam – You have been sent a notice telling you when and where to report for the examination. If the location is in a different town or otherwise unfamiliar to you, it would be well to inquire the best route and learn something about the building.
- Relax the night before the test – Allow your mind to rest. Do not study at all that night. Plan some mild recreation or diversion; then go to bed early and get a good night's sleep.
- Get up early enough to make a leisurely trip to the place for the test – This way unforeseen events, traffic snarls, unfamiliar buildings, etc. will not upset you.

- Dress comfortably – A written test is not a fashion show. You will be known by number and not by name, so wear something comfortable.
- Leave excess paraphernalia at home – Shopping bags and odd bundles will get in your way. You need bring only the items mentioned in the official notice you received; usually everything you need is provided. Do not bring reference books to the exam. They will only confuse those last minutes and be taken away from you when in the test room.
- Arrive somewhat ahead of time – If because of transportation schedules you must get there very early, bring a newspaper or magazine to take your mind off yourself while waiting.
- Locate the examination room – When you have found the proper room, you will be directed to the seat or part of the room where you will sit. Sometimes you are given a sheet of instructions to read while you are waiting. Do not fill out any forms until you are told to do so; just read them and be prepared.
- Relax and prepare to listen to the instructions
- If you have any physical problem that may keep you from doing your best, be sure to tell the test administrator. If you are sick or in poor health, you really cannot do your best on the exam. You can come back and take the test some other time.

VII. AT THE TEST

The day of the test is here and you have the test booklet in your hand. The temptation to get going is very strong. Caution! There is more to success than knowing the right answers. You must know how to identify your papers and understand variations in the type of short-answer question used in this particular examination. Follow these suggestions for maximum results from your efforts:

1) Cooperate with the monitor
The test administrator has a duty to create a situation in which you can be as much at ease as possible. He will give instructions, tell you when to begin, check to see that you are marking your answer sheet correctly, and so on. He is not there to guard you, although he will see that your competitors do not take unfair advantage. He wants to help you do your best.

2) Listen to all instructions
Don't jump the gun! Wait until you understand all directions. In most civil service tests you get more time than you need to answer the questions. So don't be in a hurry. Read each word of instructions until you clearly understand the meaning. Study the examples, listen to all announcements and follow directions. Ask questions if you do not understand what to do.

3) Identify your papers
Civil service exams are usually identified by number only. You will be assigned a number; you must not put your name on your test papers. Be sure to copy your number correctly. Since more than one exam may be given, copy your exact examination title.

4) Plan your time
Unless you are told that a test is a "speed" or "rate of work" test, speed itself is usually not important. Time enough to answer all the questions will be provided, but this

does not mean that you have all day. An overall time limit has been set. Divide the total time (in minutes) by the number of questions to determine the approximate time you have for each question.

5) Do not linger over difficult questions

If you come across a difficult question, mark it with a paper clip (useful to have along) and come back to it when you have been through the booklet. One caution if you do this – be sure to skip a number on your answer sheet as well. Check often to be sure that you have not lost your place and that you are marking in the row numbered the same as the question you are answering.

6) Read the questions

Be sure you know what the question asks! Many capable people are unsuccessful because they failed to *read* the questions correctly.

7) Answer all questions

Unless you have been instructed that a penalty will be deducted for incorrect answers, it is better to guess than to omit a question.

8) Speed tests

It is often better NOT to guess on speed tests. It has been found that on timed tests people are tempted to spend the last few seconds before time is called in marking answers at random – without even reading them – in the hope of picking up a few extra points. To discourage this practice, the instructions may warn you that your score will be "corrected" for guessing. That is, a penalty will be applied. The incorrect answers will be deducted from the correct ones, or some other penalty formula will be used.

9) Review your answers

If you finish before time is called, go back to the questions you guessed or omitted to give them further thought. Review other answers if you have time.

10) Return your test materials

If you are ready to leave before others have finished or time is called, take ALL your materials to the monitor and leave quietly. Never take any test material with you. The monitor can discover whose papers are not complete, and taking a test booklet may be grounds for disqualification.

VIII. EXAMINATION TECHNIQUES

1) Read the general instructions carefully. These are usually printed on the first page of the exam booklet. As a rule, these instructions refer to the timing of the examination; the fact that you should not start work until the signal and must stop work at a signal, etc. If there are any *special* instructions, such as a choice of questions to be answered, make sure that you note this instruction carefully.

2) When you are ready to start work on the examination, that is as soon as the signal has been given, read the instructions to each question booklet, underline any key words or phrases, such as *least, best, outline, describe*

and the like. In this way you will tend to answer as requested rather than discover on reviewing your paper that you *listed without describing*, that you selected the *worst* choice rather than the *best* choice, etc.

3) If the examination is of the objective or multiple-choice type – that is, each question will also give a series of possible answers: A, B, C or D, and you are called upon to select the best answer and write the letter next to that answer on your answer paper – it is advisable to start answering each question in turn. There may be anywhere from 50 to 100 such questions in the three or four hours allotted and you can see how much time would be taken if you read through all the questions before beginning to answer any. Furthermore, if you come across a question or group of questions which you know would be difficult to answer, it would undoubtedly affect your handling of all the other questions.

4) If the examination is of the essay type and contains but a few questions, it is a moot point as to whether you should read all the questions before starting to answer any one. Of course, if you are given a choice – say five out of seven and the like – then it is essential to read all the questions so you can eliminate the two that are most difficult. If, however, you are asked to answer all the questions, there may be danger in trying to answer the easiest one first because you may find that you will spend too much time on it. The best technique is to answer the first question, then proceed to the second, etc.

5) Time your answers. Before the exam begins, write down the time it started, then add the time allowed for the examination and write down the time it must be completed, then divide the time available somewhat as follows:
   - If 3-1/2 hours are allowed, that would be 210 minutes. If you have 80 objective-type questions, that would be an average of 2-1/2 minutes per question. Allow yourself no more than 2 minutes per question, or a total of 160 minutes, which will permit about 50 minutes to review.
   - If for the time allotment of 210 minutes there are 7 essay questions to answer, that would average about 30 minutes a question. Give yourself only 25 minutes per question so that you have about 35 minutes to review.

6) The most important instruction is to *read each question* and make sure you know what is wanted. The second most important instruction is to *time yourself properly* so that you answer every question. The third most important instruction is to *answer every question.* Guess if you have to but include something for each question. Remember that you will receive no credit for a blank and will probably receive some credit if you write something in answer to an essay question. If you guess a letter – say "B" for a multiple-choice question – you may have guessed right. If you leave a blank as an answer to a multiple-choice question, the examiners may respect your feelings but it will not add a point to your score. Some exams may penalize you for wrong answers, so in such cases *only*, you may not want to guess unless you have some basis for your answer.

7) Suggestions

    a. Objective-type questions

        1. Examine the question booklet for proper sequence of pages and questions
        2. Read all instructions carefully
        3. Skip any question which seems too difficult; return to it after all other questions have been answered
        4. Apportion your time properly; do not spend too much time on any single question or group of questions
        5. Note and underline key words – *all, most, fewest, least, best, worst, same, opposite,* etc.
        6. Pay particular attention to negatives
        7. Note unusual option, e.g., unduly long, short, complex, different or similar in content to the body of the question
        8. Observe the use of "hedging" words – *probably, may, most likely,* etc.
        9. Make sure that your answer is put next to the same number as the question
       10. Do not second-guess unless you have good reason to believe the second answer is definitely more correct
       11. Cross out original answer if you decide another answer is more accurate; do not erase until you are ready to hand your paper in
       12. Answer all questions; guess unless instructed otherwise
       13. Leave time for review

    b. Essay questions

        1. Read each question carefully
        2. Determine exactly what is wanted. Underline key words or phrases.
        3. Decide on outline or paragraph answer
        4. Include many different points and elements unless asked to develop any one or two points or elements
        5. Show impartiality by giving pros and cons unless directed to select one side only
        6. Make and write down any assumptions you find necessary to answer the questions
        7. Watch your English, grammar, punctuation and choice of words
        8. Time your answers; don't crowd material

8) Answering the essay question

Most essay questions can be answered by framing the specific response around several key words or ideas. Here are a few such key words or ideas:

M's: manpower, materials, methods, money, management
P's: purpose, program, policy, plan, procedure, practice, problems, pitfalls, personnel, public relations

    a. Six basic steps in handling problems:

        1. Preliminary plan and background development
        2. Collect information, data and facts
        3. Analyze and interpret information, data and facts
        4. Analyze and develop solutions as well as make recommendations

5. Prepare report and sell recommendations
6. Install recommendations and follow up effectiveness

b. Pitfalls to avoid
1. *Taking things for granted* – A statement of the situation does not necessarily imply that each of the elements is necessarily true; for example, a complaint may be invalid and biased so that all that can be taken for granted is that a complaint has been registered
2. *Considering only one side of a situation* – Wherever possible, indicate several alternatives and then point out the reasons you selected the best one
3. *Failing to indicate follow up* – Whenever your answer indicates action on your part, make certain that you will take proper follow-up action to see how successful your recommendations, procedures or actions turn out to be
4. *Taking too long in answering any single question* – Remember to time your answers properly

EXAMINATION SECTION

EXAMINATION SECTION
TEST 1

DIRECTIONS: Each question or incomplete statement is followed by several suggested answers or completions. Select the one that *BEST* answers the question or completes the statement. *PRINT THE LETTER OF THE CORRECT ANSWER IN THE SPACE AT THE RIGHT.*

1. A somewhat narrow intrusive formation of magma that cuts across prevailing rock structures is termed a

    A. batholith   B. sill   C. laccolith   D. dike

1.____

2. Which one of the following units represents the LONGEST period of geologic time?

    A. Epoch   B. Period   C. Age   D. Era

2.____

3. The MOST abundant metallic element in the earth's crust is

    A. aluminum   B. iron   C. magnesium   D. copper

3.____

4. Most of our knowledge concerning the structure and composition of the earth's interior has been gained from the study of which one of the following?

    A. Radio-active minerals in the earth's crust
    B. Deep-seated volcanic activity
    C. Earthquake waves
    D. Cosmic radiation

4.____

5. The study of layered rock and the reconstruction of its past history is known as which one of the following?

    A. Paleontology   B. Varvology
    C. Uniformitarianism   D. Stratigraphy

5.____

6. The ice advances and retreats during the Wisconsin Period have been MOST accurately timed by measuring the

    A. amount of silt deposited
    B. ratio of uranium to lead
    C. size of the terminal moraines
    D. ratio of carbon-14 in pieces of fossilized wood to ordinary carbon

6.____

7. Of the following, the LEAST reliable property in the identification of MOST minerals is

    A. color   B. hardness
    C. crystal form   D. chemical composition

7.____

8. Amethyst is a variety of which one of the following minerals?

    A. Beryl   B. Fluorite   C. Quartz   D. Rhondonite

8.____

9. Of the following, the one rock having a glassy appearance and which was cooled rapidly from the molten state is

    A. sandstone   B. shale   C. obsidian   D. hornblende

9.____

10. In a region of Karst topography, the underlying rock is USUALLY of which one of the following types?   10.____

    A. Granite   B. Limestone   C. Mica schist   D. Gneiss

11. Of the following, the MOST important agent of erosion of the earth's surface is   11.____

    A. wind   B. glaciers   C. running water   D. oceans

12. The GREATEST detail can be shown on a topographic map using a _____ scale and _____ contour interval.   12.____

    A. small   ;   small
    B. large   ;   large
    C. small   ;   large
    D. large   ;   small

13. Which one of the following types of air masses could be labeled mT?   13.____

    A. Warm and dry   B. Warm and moist
    C. Cold and dry   D. Cold and moist

14. Of the following, the zone in which the temperature of the atmosphere is PRACTICALLY constant is the   14.____

    A. mesophere   B. ionosphere   C. stratosphere   D. troposphere

15. A geological feature NOT associated with glaciers is a   15.____

    A. caldera   B. kame   C. drumlin   D. esker

16. The term podzolic refers specifically to a(n)   16.____

    A. type of metamorphic rock   B. oceanic deposit
    C. tektite   D. type of soil

17. The alternate light and dark colored deposits found in glacial lakes are called   17.____

    A. varves   B. kettles   C. terraces   D. tills

18. Hard water is likely to be encountered in an area whose bedrock is composed of which one of the following?   18.____

    A. Sandstone   B. Granite   C. Limestone   D. Schist

19. Which one of the features below is NOT typical of the old age phase of a river?   19.____

    A. Rapids   B. Yazoo streams   C. Meanders   D. Oxbow lakes

20. Bridal Veil Falls in California owes its presence to the fact that it is located   20.____

    A. along a line of fault
    B. along a joint line
    C. in the path of an old lava flow
    D. in a hanging valley

2

21. The boundary between the upper portion of the mantle and the lower limit of the earth's crust is known as the   21.____

    A. isostatic boundary   B. Bergschrund
    C. Moho   D. zone of deformation

22. Proof of the sphericity of the earth CANNOT be obtained by which one of the following?   22.____

    A. Observing a lunar eclipse
    B. Determining the magnetic declination at different localities along a meridian between the equator and the south pole
    C. Taking photographs of the earth from a satellite
    D. Making observations of the position of the North Star at different localities along a meridian between the equator and the north pole

23. The contour interval on a topographic map is 10 feet. The face of a steep sea cliff is shown by five closely spaced contour lines including the sea level contour. The elevation, in feet, at the top of the cliff is   23.____

    A. *exactly* 50   B. *between* 50 and 60
    C. *between* 40 and 49   D. *exactly* 40

24. On a topographic map, the GREATEST exaggeration occurs in which one of the following?   24.____

    A. Graphic scale   B. Vertical scale
    C. Horizontal scale   D. Representative fraction

25. Of the following, the fossil that is MOST commonly used as a guide in correlating oil producing areas on a worldwide basis is called   25.____

    A. Placenticeras   B. Trilobites
    C. Foraminifera   D. Cephalopods

KEY (CORRECT ANSWERS)

1.	D		11.	C
2.	D		12.	D
3.	A		13.	B
4.	C		14.	C
5.	D		15.	A
6.	D		16.	D
7.	A		17.	A
8.	C		18.	C
9.	C		19.	A
10.	B		20.	D

21.	C
22.	B
23.	C
24.	B
25.	C

TEST 2

DIRECTIONS: Each question or incomplete statement is followed by several suggested answers or completions. Select the one that *BEST* answers the question or completes the statement. *PRINT THE LETTER OF THE CORRECT ANSWER IN THE SPACE AT THE RIGHT.*

1. Amphibians arose during which one of the following times?　　　　　　　　　　1.____

   A. Mississippian　　　　　　　　　　B. Cretaceous
   C. Ordovician　　　　　　　　　　　　D. Silurian

2. The average interval, in years, between the times of the GREATEST number of sunspot　　2.____
   groups is CLOSEST to which one of the following?

   A. 7　　　　　　　B. 11　　　　　　C. 15　　　　　　D. 19

3. Natural levees, alluvial fans, and braided streams are indications of which one of the fol-　　3.____
   lowing conditions?

   A. Stream load exceeds capacity
   B. Stream load is equal to capacity
   C. Stream load is less than capacity
   D. The base level of stream erosion is dropping

4. Clay minerals are formed by chemical weathering of which one of the following groups?　　4.____

   A. Calcite and dolomite　　　　　　　B. Orthoclase and albite
   C. Varieties of quartz　　　　　　　　D. Gypsum and anhydrite

5. Of the following, the feature which CANNOT be used to infer the existence of a second　　5.____
   cycle of erosion is that of

   A. entrenched meanders　　　　　　　B. river terraces
   C. accordant hilltops　　　　　　　　　D. oxbow lakes

6. An erosional landform produced by glacial action is a　　　　　　　　　　　　6.____

   A. hogback　　　　　　　　　　　　B. cirque
   C. monadnock　　　　　　　　　　　D. natural bridge

7. Of the following, the MOST recent glacial stage was the　　　　　　　　　　　7.____

   A. Nebraskan　　　　　　　　　　　B. Wisconsin
   C. Sangamon　　　　　　　　　　　D. Kansan

8. During their geologic history the Great Lakes NEVER drained　　　　　　　　　8.____

   A. *southward* through the Mississippi
   B. *eastward* through the Mohawk and Hudson
   C. *northward* through the Red River of the North
   D. *northeastward* through the St. Lawrence

9. The degree of inclination of the beds of rock from a horizontal surface is called the　　9.____

   A. plunge　　　　B. dip　　　　C. strike　　　　D. hade

4

10. Of the common rocks, limestone is MOST easily changed by contact metamorphian because of its

    A. density   B. porosity   C. solubility   D. hardness

10.____

11. From the study of velocity and changes in intensity of earthquake waves, we know that which one of the following statements is TRUE:
The

    A. crust of the earth is between 20 and 30 miles thick on the average
    B. mantle is composed of granite
    C. core is 1,000 miles thick
    D. magma forms in the outer portion of the core

11.____

12. MOST of the mountains on the surface of the earth today are the result of which one of the following?

    A. Doming   B. Faulting
    C. Folding   D. Volcanic entrusion

12.____

13. The doctrine of uniformitarianism states that

    A. processes at work affecting the earth today are about the same as those that operated in the past
    B. the earth is the center of the solar system
    C. sedimentary rock structures follow a fixed pattern
    D. the youngest rocks are found at the top of a rock sequence

13.____

14. The MOST important source of condensation nuclei for fog and cloud formation found in nature are

    A. silver iodide   B. pollen
    C. salt   D. fine clay particles

14.____

15. Since the pressure force is perpendicular to the isobars and the deflecting force caused by the earth's rotation is opposite to the pressure force, it follows that a wind above the friction level will blow

    A. at right angles to the isobars
    B. parallel to the isobars
    C. in the direction of the low pressure area
    D. in opposition to the Coriolis force

15.____

16. How many calories of heat energy are released when 1 kilogram of water vapor at a temperature of zero degrees C condenses and then turns to ice at zero degrees C?

    A. 54,000   B. 80,000   C. 620,000   D. 800,000

16.____

17. Radiation type ground fogs are ALWAYS accompanied by a

    A. greater than normal lapse rate
    B. moist adiabatic lapse rate
    C. marked temperature inversion
    D. pseudoadiabatic lapse rate

17.____

18. The occurrence of waterfalls in stream-valley history is a mark of   18.____

    A. youth   B. early maturity
    C. late maturity   D. old age

19. Which one of the following mountain ranges are mature?   19.____

    A. Adirondacks   B. Himalayas
    C. Sierra Nevadas   D. Rockies

20. Which one of the following terms BEST describes the Catskill mountains?   20.____

    A. Complex mountains   B. Block-fault mountains
    C. Domed mountains   D. Dissected plateau

21. Which one of the following minerals is MOST resistant to chemical weathering?   21.____

    A. Feldspar   B. Gypsum   C. Talc   D. Quartz

22. Molten rock which solidifies below the surface of the earth is called   22.____

    A. intrusive   B. extrusive   C. metamorphic   D. sedimentary

23. Which one of the following is used to designate the high land between two river systems?   23.____
A

    A. terrace   B. plateau   C. tor   D. divide

24. At which one of the following periods are both ends of the earth's axis equidistant from   24.____
the sun?

    A. Every day of the year
    B. Only during the summer solstice
    C. Only during the winter solstice
    D. Only during the equinoxes

25. Which one of the following is considered the MOST probable cause of the Aurora Borea-   25.____
lis?

    A. Electrically charged particles from the sun
    B. Reflection of light rays from snowfields
    C. Dispersion of light by prismatic effects of ice crystals
    D. Refraction of moonlight

KEY (CORRECT ANSWERS)

1.	C		11.	A
2.	B		12.	C
3.	A		13.	A
4.	B		14.	C
5.	D		15.	B
6.	B		16.	C
7.	B		17.	C
8.	C		18.	A
9.	B		19.	A
10.	C		20.	D

21.	D
22.	A
23.	D
24.	D
25.	A

TEST 3

DIRECTIONS: Each question or incomplete statement is followed by several suggested answers or completions. Select the one that *BEST* answers the question or completes the statement. *PRINT THE LETTER OF THE CORRECT ANSWER IN THE SPACE AT THE RIGHT.*

1. Granite is a rock that was made from which one of the following?   1._____

   A. Cooling of lava from volcanoes
   B. Cooling of lava deep beneath the earth's surface
   C. Compression of sediments
   D. Cementation of sediments

2. Besides temperature, which one of the following factors determines the nature of a meta-   2._____
   morphic rock?

   A. Pressure
   B. Erosion of overlying sediments
   C. Pressure and composition of fluids that permeate rocks
   D. Pressure and erosion of overlying sediments

3. At which one of the following seasons of the northern hemisphere of the earth is the   3._____
   earth FARTHEST from the sun?

   A. Autumn   B. Spring   C. Summer   D. Winter

4. With which one of the following are active volcanoes USUALLY associated?   4._____

   A. Dissected plateaus   B. Glaciated areas
   C. Peneplanes   D. Young mountains

5. The YOUNGEST bedrock found in New York City is which one of the following?   5._____

   A. Mica schist   B. Dolomite   C. Gneiss   D. Marble

6. If a mine foreman is brought to the surface, which is at an elevation of 300 ft. above sea   6._____
   level, from a mine, which is 1,250 feet below sea level, an aneroid barometer in his pos-
   session would show a(n) _____ of _____ inches.

   A. *decrease*   ;   1 1/2
   B. *decrease*   ;   3
   C. *increase*   ;   1 1/2
   D. *increase*   ;   3

7. Columnar structure found in many volcanic necks will form according to which one of the   7._____
   following sets of patterns and conditions?

   A. Parallel to the lava surface, accompanied by slow cooling
   B. Parallel to the lava surface, accompanied by rapid cooling
   C. At right angles to the lava surface, accompanied by slow cooling
   D. At right angles to the lava surface, accompanied by rapid cooling

8. Of the following, which one rock will permit the EASIEST movement of ground water?   8._____

   A. Basalt   B. Conglomerate   C. Granite   D. Quartzite

9. Of the following, the one element MOST evenly represented in sea water, river water, and rock is

    A. silica   B. chlorine   C. calcium   D. magnesium

9.____

10. Of the following, the mineral which can be scratched by a fingernail is

    A. feldspar   B. hornblende   C. mica   D. quartz

10.____

11. All crystals which have three axes of the same length and at right angles to each other belong to which one of the following systems?

    A. Monoclinic   B. Isometric   C. Rhombic   D. Orthorhombic

11.____

12. Which one of the following is MOST representative of lake deposits?

    A. Sands and talus   B. Sands and gravels
    C. Sands and clays   D. Clays and silts

12.____

13. In strongly meandering streams the deepest water is USUALLY found in which of the following regions? _____ along the _____ curve.

    A. *Upstream*   ;   outer
    B. *Upstream*   ;   inner
    C. *Downstream* ;   outer
    D. *Downstream* ;   inner

13.____

14. An esker is a deposit formed by which one of the following?

    A. Running water   B. Shore currents
    C. Weathering   D. Wind

14.____

15. Isoseismic lines on a map connect points that are equal in which one of the following?

    A. Intensity of earthquake shocks
    B. Variation of magnetic force
    C. Metamorphosis of rock in contact with magma
    D. Temperature

15.____

16. Of the following, which one is an instrument used to study the composition of stars?

    A. Chronometer   B. Seismograph
    C. Sextant   D. Spectroscope

16.____

17. Of the following rocks, which one is MOST easily weathered by freezing and thawing?

    A. Limestone   B. Obsidian
    C. Quartzite   D. Sandstone

17.____

18. Among the following, the one planet whose orbit has the GREATEST eccentricity is

    A. Mercury   B. Jupiter   C. Mars   D. Pluto

18.____

19. The spectra of the more distant galaxies show spectrum lines at greater wavelengths than normal.
The interpretation usually given to these spectrum lines is that the distance between galaxies is

    A. *decreasing* steadily   B. *decreasing* intermittently
    C. *increasing* steadily   D. *increasing* intermittently

19.____

20. The existence of fossil corals indicates that in addition to clean water, which one of the   20.____
following sets of conditions prevailed at the time of their formation?

    A. Deep, cool, fresh water
    B. Shallow, warm, fresh water
    C. Shallow, cool, marine water
    D. Shallow, warm, marine water

21. The SMALLEST number of elements which together comprise 99% of the earth's crust is   21.____

    A. 8   B. 18   C. 80   D. 98

22. Of the following groups, which one represents ONLY the constructive work of ground   22.____
water?

    A. Stalagmite, helictite, travertine, natural bridge
    B. Helictite, travertine, natural bridge, stalactite
    C. Travertine, natural bridge, staclactite, stalagmite
    D. Travertine, helictite, column, stalagmite

23. Which one of the following problems has been MAINLY solved in Paleontology?   23.____
The

    A. stratigraphic and geographic occurrence of fossil organisms and the range in varia-
       tion in fossil materials
    B. actual environment of most fossil assemblages
    C. time, place, and manner in which different animal groups developed hard parts
    D. relative age of rock units and fossils over most of the earth

24. Which one of the following sets of minerals have rhombohedral cleavage?   24.____

    A. Halite and galena
    B. Dolomite and calcite
    C. Feldspar and hornblende
    D. Sphalerite and mica

25. The SMALLEST daily temperature ranges are MOST likely to occur at which one of the   25.____
following regions?

    A. Arctic circle   B. Equator
    C. North Pole   D. Tropic of Cancer

KEY (CORRECT ANSWERS)

1.	B		11.	B
2.	C		12.	D
3.	C		13.	C
4.	D		14.	A
5.	A		15.	A
6.	A		16.	D
7.	C		17.	D
8.	B		18.	D
9.	D		19.	C
10.	C		20.	D

21.	A
22.	D
23.	D
24.	B
25.	C

———

TEST 4

DIRECTIONS: Each question or incomplete statement is followed by several suggested answers or completions. Select the one that *BEST* answers the question or completes the statement. *PRINT THE LETTER OF THE CORRECT ANSWER IN THE SPACE AT THE RIGHT.*

1. Fossil remains indicate that the course of evolution of organisms on the earth has been which one of the following?   1.____

   A. A continuous straight line evolution
   B. Advance in large and sudden jumps
   C. Development of greater complexity at a specific rate
   D. Radiation of organisms in many directions

2. At the present time MOST species are classified on the basis of   2.____

   A. genetic structures
   B. homologous compatability
   C. physiological characteristics
   D. cytological resemblances

3. Of the following, the one which is characteristic of youthful streams is that they   3.____
   A. have meanders   B. are graded
   C. have rapids   D. flow on flood plains

4. The Ewing-Donn hypothesis attempts to explain   4.____

   A. mountain building   B. the origin of the earth
   C. ice ages   D. the origin of life on earth

5. The two MOST abundant chemical elements in the earth's crust are   5.____

   A. oxygen and silicon   B. oxygen and hydrogen
   C. silicon and aluminum   D. silicon and iron

6. Taconite is a low-grade ore of   6.____

   A. nickel   B. iron   C. titanium   D. copper

7. The type of rock MOST commonly found in batholiths is   7.____

   A. basalt   B. granite   C. felsite   D. gabbro

8. The Great Salt Lake of Utah is the remnant of a much larger fresh-water lake of Pleistocene times called Lake   8.____

   A. Agassiz   B. Lahontan   C. Bonneville   D. Algonquin

9. Which one of the following minerals is ALSO a native element?   9.____

   A. Galena   B. Gypsum   C. Graphite   D. Garnet

10. The type of coal MOST likely to be found in strata that were deeply buried and strongly folded is   10.____

    A. bituminous coal   B. lignite
    C. anthracite   D. peat

11. A common accessory mineral in the mica schist of Manhattan Island is   11.____

    A. garnet   B. magnetite   C. diopside   D. olivine

12. Of the following, the MOST likely reason for the failure of geologists to find fossils in the bed rock of Manhattan Island is that   12.____

    A. living organisms were scarce at the time of formation of the rocks
    B. any possible remains of life were obliterated by metamorphism
    C. fossil-bearing layers are deeply buried beneath alluvium and glacial deposits
    D. little search has been made for them

13. Glacial striations on exposed bedrock outcrops in New York City strike   13.____

    A. NW-SE   B. N-S   C. W-E   D. NE-SW

14. An igneous intrusion which causes doming of the overlying sedimentary rocks is known as a   14.____

    A. batholith   B. dike   C. volcanic neck   D. laccolith

15. Eskers are depositional features which have the shape of   15.____

    A. broad, flat-topped hills
    B. dome-like mounds
    C. narrow, winding ridges
    D. rectilinear escarpments

16. An erosional remnant on a peneplane is called a   16.____

    A. roche moutonee   B. monadnock   C. nunatak   D. stack

17. A rhumb line on the earth's surface is ALWAYS a(the)   17.____

    A. line of constant bearing
    B. segment of a great circle
    C. segment of a small circle
    D. shortest distance between two points

18. Of the following, the form of vegetation MOST typical of the tundra is the   18.____

    A. dwarf pine   B. cactus   C. moss   D. sagebrush

19. The first IMPORTANT record of fossil land plants is found in rocks of which one of the following periods?   19.____

    A. Devonian   B. Triassic   C. Cambrian   D. Cretaceous

20. Of the following, the type of soil which absorbs water MOST slowly is   20.____

    A. loam   B. sand   C. humus   D. clay

21. Of the following, the one which is an example of an alluvial plain is a(n) _____ plain.   21.____

    A. lava   B. till   C. outwash   D. delta

22. Lines drawn on a map through points of equal pressure are called   22.____

    A. divides   B. isobars
    C. isotherms   D. contour lines

23. The OLDEST type of map projection is the   23.____

    A. Mercator   B. Gnomonic
    C. Lambert conformal   D. Polyconic

24. Level areas are indicated on a contour map by contour lines which   24.____

    A. are close together   B. are far apart
    C. coincide   D. are circular or oval

25. Compared with a land area, a water area heats more_____ and cools more _____.   25.____

    A. *rapidly* ; *rapidly*
    B. *rapidly* ; *slowly*
    C. *slowly* ; *rapidly*
    D. *slowly* ; *slowly*

KEY (CORRECT ANSWERS)

1.	D		11.	A
2.	B		12.	B
3.	C		13.	A
4.	C		14.	D
5.	A		15.	C
6.	B		16.	B
7.	B		17.	A
8.	C		18.	C
9.	C		19.	A
10.	C		20.	D

21.	D
22.	B
23.	A
24.	B
25.	D

TEST 5

DIRECTIONS: Each question or incomplete statement is followed by several suggested answers or completions. Select the one that *BEST* answers the question or completes the statement. *PRINT THE LETTER OF THE CORRECT ANSWER IN THE SPACE AT THE RIGHT.*

1. All of the following statements concerning artesian wells are TRUE EXCEPT that

    A. they usually provide much larger quantities of water than ordinary wells
    B. their main source of water is local rainfall
    C. in general, the farther they are from their outcrops, the deeper their aquifer
    D. the water in the aquifers is under pressure

1.____

2. A speleologist is a

    A. cave explorer   B. space explorer
    C. weather forecaster   D. mountain climber

2.____

3. The use of which one of the following is the MOST accurate way of dating relatively recent fossils?

    A. Concentration of salt in the sea
    B. Rate of deposition of river sediment
    C. Half-life of radioactive carbon
    D. Uranium-lead ratio

3.____

4. Through the measurement of the fluorine and nitrogen contents of fossil bones, scientists have shown that which one of the following fossil men is a hoax?

    A. Pithecanthropus   B. Sinanthropus
    C. Piltdown   D. Australopithecus

4.____

5. The rugged, deeply embayed shoreline of New England was formed by

    A. volcanic activity accompanied by regional faulting
    B. the uplift of a submerged peneplane
    C. the subsidence of a well-dissected region
    D. wave attack upon glacial and glacio-fluvial deposits

5.____

6. An animal thought to have become extinct some 60 million years ago has been discovered still living in the ocean off the coast of Madagascar.
   It belongs to the group known as

    A. coelacanths   B. trilobites
    C. graptolites   D. plesiosaurs

6.____

7. The contact between the Cretaceous marine sediments and the crystalline metamorphic rocks of New York City beneath Long Island may be described as

    A. conformable   B. gradational
    C. unconformable   D. faulted

7.____

8. A rock of igneous origin occurring in New York City and vicinity is which one of the following?

    A. Muscovite schist   B. Dolomitic marble
    C. Arkose sandstone   D. Granite pegmatite

8.____

9. Abandoned magnetite mines in the Adirondack Mountains have been re-activated in recent years for the recovery of   9.____

   A. iron   B. titanium   C. copper   D. lead

10. Of the following conditions, the one which would prevent the periodic eruption of a geyser is   10.____

   A. an intricate underground fracture system
   B. subterranean heat
   C. a plentiful supply of ground water
   D. contact of the ground water with molten rock below the surface

11. Which one of the following elements may be called a native element?   11.____

   A. Phosphorus   B. Sulfur   C. Potassium   D. Chlorine

12. The much publicized *Mohole* is an undertaking designed to   12.____

   A. discover more petroleum reserves
   B. explore recently discovered mineral deposits
   C. obtain information on the conditions prevailing at the base of the earth's crust
   D. tap a reservoir of magma in the earth's crust

13. The base level of erosion is the   13.____

   A. line along which a stream becomes graded
   B. water table
   C. first resistant stratum the stream reaches
   D. limit of downward erosion by running water

14. It is INCORRECT to state that a loccolith   14.____

   A. is extrusive in origin
   B. has a flat floor
   C. is a concordant igneous intrusion
   D. has caused doming of the overlying rock layers

15. A pebble which is in part well-rounded and in part sub-angular was MOST likely abraded by the action of   15.____

   A. wind   B. waves   C. glaciers   D. streams

16. The second MOST abundant element in the earth's crust is   16.____

   A. Al   B. Ca   C. Na   D. Si

17. Of the following common minerals, the one which MOST successfully resists weathering is   17.____

   A. quartz   B. calcite   C. hornblende   D. orthoclase

18. Gneiss is a(n)   18.____

    A. intrusive igneous rock exhibiting a streaky alignment of minerals
    B. stratified sedimentary rock
    C. metamorphic rock with a banded structure
    D. metamorphic rock with a massive, non-foliated structure

19. Of the following, the rock structure which is the result of metamorphism is   19.____

    A. columnar structure   B. stratification
    C. vesicular structure   D. foliation

20. The radioactive method which CANNOT be used to determine rock ages in excess of   20.____
50,000 years involves the radioactive decay of an isotope of which one of the following
elements?

    A. Potassium   B. Carbon   C. Strontium   D. Thorium

21. Orogenic movements in the earth's crust are responsible for the formation of which one   21.____
of the following?

    A. Folded mountain ranges
    B. Geosynclines
    C. Elevated marine terraces
    D. Submerged shorelines

22. Accepted inferences concerning the layered structure of the earth's interior are   22.____
LARGELY based on

    A. calculations of the average density of the earth
    B. gravimetric measurements from submarines
    C. measurements of the earth's magnetic field
    D. sharp changes in travel time of earthquake waves at certain depths

23. A meandering stream flows MOST rapidly   23.____

    A. near the undercut bank   B. near the slip-off slope
    C. near the center   D. at the bottom

24. An erosional remnant produced by the action of waves along a shore is called a   24.____

    A. col   B. stack   C. roche moutonnee   D. kame

25. Of the following, which structure CANNOT be classified as a fold?   25.____

    A. Homocline   B. Anticline   C. Monocline   D. Syncline

KEY (CORRECT ANSWERS)

1.	B	11.	B
2.	A	12.	C
3.	C	13.	D
4.	C	14.	A
5.	C	15.	C
6.	A	16.	D
7.	C	17.	A
8.	D	18.	C
9.	B	19.	D
10.	D	20.	B

21. A
22. D
23. A
24. B
25. A

EXAMINATION SECTION
TEST 1

DIRECTIONS: Each question or incomplete statement is followed by several suggested answers or completions. Select the one that *BEST* answers the question or completes the statement. *PRINT THE LETTER OF THE CORRECT ANSWER IN THE SPACE AT THE RIGHT.*

1. Rock fragments at the base of a steep slope form

    A. talus   B. moraines   C. kames   D. geodes

    1._____

2. The most important activity of a mature river is

    A. downcutting   B. headward erosion
    C. deposition   D. widening its valley

    2._____

3. Among the following, the one which is a common mineral that replaces organic sub-stances in fossil formation is

    A. $CaSO_4$ B. Na_2CO_3 C. SiO_2 D. SiO_3

    3._____

4. The most common mineral in the earth's crust is

    A. mica   B. feldspar   C. hornblende   D. calcite

    4._____

5. Niagara Falls has a limestone cap underlaid by

    A. shale   B. granite   C. basalt   D. schist

    5._____

6. The theory that mountains and plains maintain a state of balance by slow vertical adjust-ment is known as

    A. isostasy   B. isomerism
    C. isomorphism   D. isotopism

    6._____

7. The Devil's Tower in Wyoming is an example of a(n)

    A. erratic   B. stock
    C. monadnock   D. volcanic neck

    7._____

8. Of the following, a volcano that *BEST* illustrates a composite cone is

    A. Mauna Loa   B. Paricutin
    C. Vesuvius   D. Kilauea

    8._____

9. The feature below that is most useful in indicating the direction of movement of a conti-nental glacier is the

    A. arete   B. cirque   C. kettle hole   D. drumlin

    9._____

10. Sinkhole lakes would be found most readily in which one of the following states?

    A. New York   B. Florida
    C. Minnesota   D. Massachusetts

    10._____

11. The Sierra Nevada mountains were produced primarily by   11.____

     A. folding   B. igneous intrusion
     C. volcanic eruptions   D. faulting

12. Of the following agents of erosion, the one that produces limestone caves is   12.____

     A. ocean waves   B. wind
     C. ground water   D. surface streams

13. The most recent covering of New England by continental glaciers ended at a time closest   13.____
to which one of the following?

     A. 10,000 B.C.   B. 100,000 B.C.
     C. 200,000 B.C.   D. 400,000 B.C.

14. The earliest deposits of graphite left by simple forms of life resulted from such life in   14.____
which one of the following eras?

     A. Cenozoic   B. Archeozoic
     C. Mesozoic   D. Paleozoic

15. The study of radioactive minerals shows the earth to have a minimum age, in years, clos-   15.____
est to which one of the following?

     A. 50,000   B. 500,000
     C. 5,000,000   D. 5,000,000,000

16. The texture of an igneous rock is determined primarily by   16.____

     A. chemical composition   B. rate of cooling
     C. age   D. density

17. Shale may metamorphose into   17.____

     A. quartzite   B. marble
     C. anthracite coal   D. slate

18. Of the following, the mineral most resistant to both chemical and mechanical weathering   18.____
is

     A. calcite   B. mica   C. quartz   D. feldspar

19. Which one of the following is *NOT* a star classification?   19.____

     A. White dwarfs   B. Red giants
     C. Green giants   D. Red variables

20. Which one of the following is the minimum average monthly temperature required for a   20.____
zone to be considered tropical?

     A. 54° F   B. 64° F   C. 74° F   D. 84° F

21. Which one of the following is the name given to lines on a weather map connecting   21.____
points of equal barometric pressure?

     A. Isobars   B. Isomers   C. Isotopes   D. Isotherms

22. Which arrangement below is typical of a lunar eclipse?   22._____

   A. Moon between earth and sun
   B. Earth between moon and sun
   C. Sun between moon and earth
   D. Dense clouds between earth and moon

23. Of the following, which statement about auroras is *LEAST* accurate?   23._____

   A. They occur near the poles only.
   B. They are caused by ionization of oxygen and nitrogen in the upper air.
   C. They are at their brightest during maximum sunspot activity.
   D. They are at their brightest during full moon.

24. Of the following, which one is closest to the distance, in miles, from the earth to the moon?   24._____

   A. 2.5×10^3 B. 2.5×10^4
   C. 2.5×10^5 D. 2.5×10^6

25. When flying along which one of the following is a plane on a great circle route?   25._____

   A. The Tropic of Capricorn   B. Any rhumb line
   C. A meridian   D. The Arctic Circle

26. Of the following, which lunar feature is *NOT* truly described by its name?   26._____

   A. Mountain   B. Sea   C. Crater   D. Valley

27. Boothbay Maine is characterized by its   27._____

   A. barrier beaches   B. lagoons
   C. long narrow bays   D. regular coastline

28. Streams tend to swerve to the right in the northern hemisphere in accordance with Ferrel's law. This deflecting force would be greatest at which one of the following latitudes?   28._____

   A. the equator   B. 30 degrees N.
   C. 60 degrees N.   D. 80 degrees N.

29. Of the following volcanoes, the one known in the 20th century for its most violently explosive type of eruption is   29._____

   A. Mt. Lassen, Cal.   B. Mt. Pelee, Martinique
   C. Mt. Vesuvius, Italy   D. Paricutin, Mexico

30. The star nearest to the sun is in the constellation,   30._____

   A. Capricornus   B. Centaurus
   C. Sagittarius   D. Ursa Major

31. When it is 3 P.M. standard time in New York City, the city, among the following, in which it is 8 P.M. standard time is   31._____

   A. Honolulu, Hawaii   B. London, England
   C. Nome, Alaska   D. Moscow, Russia

21

32. At the summer solstice, the vertical rays of the sun at noon are on the   32.____

    A. equator   B. parallel of 15 north
    C. Tropic of Cancer   D. Tropic of Capricorn

33. The reason why the period of the Earth's rotation has been increasing is that   33.____

    A. the moon's orbit has been increasing
    B. frictional heat is produced in the atmosphere
    C. tides produce a drag
    D. the Earth has been cooling down

34. Of the following, the cloud formation that consists entirely of ice crystals is   34.____

    A. cumulus   B. nimbus   C. stratus   D. cirrus

35. When a glaciated valley is undercut below sea level, it is called a   35.____

    A. tidal race   B. tidal bore
    C. fjord   D. cirque

36. A pale gray, non-crystalline rock, which contains many small shells of marine animals, and which dissolves slowly in carbonic acid is probably   36.____

    A. shale   B. sandstone   C. limestone   D. granite

37. Dendritic drainage is characteristic of which one of the following?   37.____

    A. Coastal plains in the mature stage
    B. Plains of essentially homogeneous rocks
    C. Domed areas
    D. Volcanoes

38. Extensive mud stone and silt stone deposits indicate that deposition probably occured in which one of the following areas?   38.____

    A. In low-lying land source areas
    B. In blow holes
    C. Along steep coastal areas
    D. In front of mountain ranges

39. A river meander migrates as a result of which one of the following?   39.____

    A. Retreat of cut-bank and advance of slip-off slope
    B. Retreat of cut-bank
    C. Advance of slip-off slope
    D. Retreat of cut-bank, advance of slip-off slope and downstream erosion

40. A mature river will become intrenched when the area in which it is located is which one of the following?   40.____

    A. Flooded   B. Peneplaned
    C. Elevated   D. Lowered

41. Fall Line cities are located where rivers flow from the rocks of 41.____

    A. newer Appalachians to those of the older Appalachians
    B. older Appalachians to those of the coastal plain
    C. coastal plain into the Atlantic Ocean
    D. Appalachian plateau to the rocks of the newer Appalachian

42. Most Cenozoic mammal fossils were preserved by 42.____

    A. burial after drowning or suffocation
    B. mummification
    C. volcanic ash
    D. trapping in caves

43. The skull of Pithecanthropus erectus differs from that of an ape in that the former pre-sents which one of the following features? 43.____

    A. Lack of a median crest
    B. No prominent bony ridges over the eye orbits
    C. A slightly smaller brain cavity than a full-grown gorilla
    D. No brain convolutions

44. Baltic amber contains large numbers of which one of the following fossilized remains? 44.____

    A. Worms   B. Insects
    C. Cephalopods   D. Crinoids

45. Of the following, the one in which the greatest variety of species is found is 45.____

    A. cretaceous chalk   B. Cenozoic angiosperms
    C. Eocene algae   D. Cenozoic protozoa

46. Of the following, the primate which *LEAST* resembles man in structure is the 46.____

    A. chimpanzee   B. lemur   C. gorilla   D. gibbon

47. The triangulation point on a topographic map shows 47.____

    A. latitude and longitude   B. true elevation
    C. magnetic declination   D. true north

48. Of the following, a heavy black line on a geologic map, with the letters U and D appearing on opposite sides of the line, is the symbol for a(n) 48.____

    A. unconformity   B. plunging anticline
    C. overtuned fold   D. fault

49. On a geologic map, the symbol T 30 indicates 49.____

    A. strike N-S; dip 30° E.
    B. dip E-W; strike 30° N.
    C. strike E-W; dip 30° S.
    D. strike E-W; dip 30° N.

50. If the direction of a sight line from a fire tower to a column of smoke indicating the start of   50.____
a forest fire has a magnetic compass bearing N 25° W, and if the magnetic declination of
the locality is 12° E, the true direction which must be plotted on the map, in order to
locate the trouble spot, is which one of the following?

A. N 13° E   B. N 13° W
C. N 37° W   D. N 37° E

———————

KEY (CORRECT ANSWERS)

1. A	11. D	21. A	31. B	41. B
2. D	12. C	22. B	32. C	42. A
3. C	13. A	23. D	33. C	43. A
4. B	14. B	24. C	34. D	44. B
5. A	15. D	25. C	35. C	45. D
6. A	16. B	26. B	36. C	46. B
7. D	17. D	27. C	37. B	47. B
8. C	18. C	28. D	38. A	48. D
9. D	19. C	29. B	39. D	49. C
10. B	20. B	30. B	40. C	50. B

———————

TEST 2

DIRECTIONS: Each question or incomplete statement is followed by several suggested answers or completions. Select the one that *BEST* answers the question or completes the statement. *PRINT THE LETTER OF THE CORRECT ANSWER IN THE SPACE AT THE RIGHT.*

1. The moon revolves about the earth at a speed (in miles per hour) closest to   1.____

    A. 2000   B. 7000   C. 18,000   D. 25,000

2. Through approximately how many degrees of latitude do the vertical rays of the sun move from January 1 of one year to January 1 of the next year?   2.____

    A. 23 1/2   B. 47   C. 94   D. 180

3. Which one of the following represents the highest rate of revolution, in miles per hour?   3.____

    A. The earth at perihelion
    B. The earth at aphelion
    C. The moon at perigee
    D. The moon at apogee

4. Which one of the following depositional features is characterized by a high degree of sorting of its component particles?   4.____

    A. Alluvial fan   B. Delta
    C. Ground moraine   D. Talus slope

5. A column of air that has a lapse rate of 7.5° F per 1000 feet is   5.____

    A. absolutely stable   B. conditionally unstable
    C. stable   D. unstable

6. The name given to the process whereby rocks are altered due to the exchange of ions is   6.____

    A. microscism   B. lithification
    C. metasomatism   D. metamorphism

7. The symbol mTk appears on a weather map over the southeastern United States in summer. The characteristic *MOST LIKELY* to be associated with it is   7.____

    A. poor visibility   B. stratiform clouds
    C. thunderstorms   D. low humidity

8. What is the approximate altitude of a plane in which a barometer reads 843 millibars when a sea level barometer reads 1013 mb.?   8.____

    A. 1000'   B. 2000'   C. 3000'   D. 5000'

9. Aberration of starlight is regarded as evidence of the   9.____

    A. earth's revolution around the sun
    B. earth's rotation on its axis
    C. earth's spheroidal shape
    D. existence of the earth's magnetic field

10. The cyclic nature of the processes by which our planet is eroded and carved, only to be   10.____
reelevated and the cycle to begin again, was first clearly presented by

    A. Aristotle   B. Louis Agassiz
    C. James Hutton   D. A.K. Lobeck

11. Chemical weathering is likely to be the dominant weathering process in regions having a   11.____
climate that is

    A. moist, cold   B. dry, warm
    C. moist, warm   D. dry, cold

12. The stage of dissection of a region is determined on the basis of   12.____

    A. type of drainage pattern present
    B. kinds of rocks underlying the region
    C. amount of material removed by erosion in relation to volume present before dissection
    D. type of erosional agent responsible for the dissection

13. Where stream capture has occurred, the feature which may develop in the pirated stream   13.____
course is a(n)

    A. increased volume   B. increased velocity
    C. barbed tributaries   D. wind gap

14. Of the following, the main feature formed by a river after it has attained its profile of equi-   14.____
librium is a

    A. canyon   B. waterfall
    C. deep channel   D. flood plain

15. Of the following, the one that does NOT produce deposition of minerals by ground water   15.____
is

    A. evaporation
    B. reduction of temperature
    C. addition of dissolved minerals
    D. increase in temperature

16. An entrenched meander occurs as a consequence of   16.____

    A. headward erosion
    B. differential weathering
    C. vertical uplift
    D. shifting of the stream bed

17. Which one of the following processes is responsible for MOST of the geologic work   17.____
accomplished by ground water?

    A. Abrasion   B. Solution
    C. Hydraulic action   D. Oxidation

18. The artesian wells of southern Long Island are fed by water that enters the ground *PRINCIPALLY* in

    A. the locality of the wells
    B. northern Long Island
    C. southern Connecticut
    D. the Catskills

18.____

19. In order to yield a maximum amount of water in the minimum time, a well should be drilled in rocks which are

    A. porous and permeable
    B. porous and impermeable
    C. non-porous and permeable
    D. non-porous and impermeable

19.____

20. The coast of southern Long Island is classified as a

    A. shoreline of emergence   B. submerged coast
    C. neutral shoreline   D. compound shoreline

20.____

21. Sandbars are *MOST LIKELY* to appear in the bed of a river

    A. on the outside curve of a meander
    B. where the slope increases rapidly
    C. at a place where the river widens
    D. regions rejuvenated by uplift

21.____

22. The Niagara River Gorge is approximately 300 ft. deep, despite the fact that the falls are only about 160 ft. above the water. This seeming discrepancy is due to

    A. diastrophic action along the river course
    B. sinking of the limestone bed
    C. formation of a plungepool at the base of the falls
    D. formation of potholes from the rapids

22.____

23. Of the following, the one region with the *MOST* extensive plains in the world is

    A. central India   B. Australia
    C. northern Siberia   D. the Amazon basin

23.____

24. Of the following, the feature that *CANNOT* be used as evidence for faulting is

    A. slickensides   B. displacement of beds
    C. cross-bedding   D. dragging of beds

24.____

25. The Sierra Nevada is a mountain chain formed *PRINCIPALLY* by

    A. folding
    B. volcanic eruptions
    C. block faulting
    D. erosion of horizontal strata

25.____

26. Plateaus can *ALWAYS* be distinguished from mountains on the basis of

    A. elevation   B. depth of valleys
    C. rock structure   D. faulting

26.____

27. The theory of earth movements advanced by Wegener is known as the   27._____

    A. Contraction Theory
    B. Continental Drift Theory
    C. Convection Hypothesis
    D. Theory of Gravitational Sliding

28. Which one of the following topographic quadrangles would be *BEST* for showing water   28._____
gaps?

    A. Bright Angel, Arizona
    B. Donaldsonville, Louisiana
    C. Harrisburg, Pennsylvania
    D. Niagara Gorge, New York

29. Thrust faults are the result of   29._____

    A. isostatic movements
    B. tensional forces
    C. compressional forces
    D. movements of the sea level

30. The general rule that younger rocks lie on top of older rocks is known as the law of   30._____

    A. horizontality   B. superposition
    C. consequence   D. competence

31. The slopes of surfaces of aggradation are usually steepest on   31._____

    A. flood plains   B. river bars
    C. alluvial fans   D. talus cones

32. The Catskills of New York State are classified structurally as   32._____

    A. an extension of the New England peneplane
    B. domed mountains
    C. a mature dissected plateau
    D. part of the Appalachian ridge and valley region

33. Pittsburgh, Pa., lies in the physiographic province known as the   33._____

    A. Triassic Lowland   B. Folded Appalachians
    C. Appalachian Plateau   D. Atlantic Coastal Plain

34. The rocks in the vicinity of New York, New Jersey and Connecticut which contain the   34._____
remains of dinosaurs are in the

    A. Atlantic Coastal Plain   B. Jurassic Lowlands
    C. Triassic Lowlands   D. Cretaceous Lowlands

35. An unconformity is the line of contact between   35._____

    A. displaced horizontal layers
    B. rocks on both sides of a thrust fault
    C. rocks of different ages of the earth's history
    D. unconsolidated material and sedimentary rock

36. Of the following national parks, which one exhibits the *BEST* exposed evidences of past valley glaciation?   36.____

    A. Yellowstone   B. Mt. Ranier
    C. Yosemite   D. Crater Lake

37. The topography of the present Columbia River region in the State of Washington was formed by the dissection of a   37.____

    A. huge granite batholith
    B. thick sequence of tilted limestones
    C. wide belt of folded, metamorphic rocks
    D. series of fissure flows of basalt

38. Deep canyons are characteristic of   38.____

    A. young plateaus
    B. maturely dissected plateaus
    C. old plateaus
    D. peneplanes

39. Slaty cleavage is developed in an attitude which is most nearly   39.____

    A. parallel to the bedding
    B. vertical
    C. horizontal
    D. parallel to the axial planes of the folds

40. Since about 1860, glaciers in general around the world appear to be   40.____

    A. maintaining their size
    B. maintaining their size and position
    C. shrinking and receding
    D. advancing but maintaining their size

41. An example of a former glacial lake of large size which left a broad lake plain is   41.____

    A. Lake Bonneville   B. Lake Agassiz
    C. Lake Pontchartrain   D. Great Salt Lake

42. Of the following, the *BEST* evidence for the epeirogenic uplift of the Grand Canyon region of the Colorado River, which elevated its rims to a position 7500 feet above sea level, is the   42.____

    A. depth of the present Canyon, exceeding 5000 feet
    B. intense folding of the Paleozoic rocks exposed in the Canyon walls
    C. presence of marine fossils in the unfolded rim rocks (Kaibab limestone)
    D. intense metamorphism of the Pre-Cambrian rocks exposed in the walls of the Inner Gorge

43. Hanging valleys may occur where a   43.____

    A. mountain region has undergone glaciation
    B. plateau has been maturely dissected
    C. shoreline has been recently submerged
    D. stream has been rejuvenated

44. Of the following glacial deposits, the one that will show some degree of stratification is the   44._____

    A. terminal moraine   B. esker
    C. drumlin   D. ground moraine

45. The projection used for U.S. Geological Survey topographic maps is the   45._____

    A. Mercator   B. Polyconic
    C. Orthographic   D. Azimuthal Equidistant

46. Slope (in feet per mile) can be determined from a topographic map by using the   46._____

    A. contour interval and scale of miles
    B. elevation and contour interval
    C. direction and scale of miles
    D. distance between two adjacent contour lines

47. Of the following statements, the one that is *NOT* true of clay minerals is that a clay mineral   47._____

    A. has a characteristic space lattice
    B. is formed by weathering or alteration of a pre-existing mineral
    C. is stable under a wide range of pressures and temperatures
    D. crystallizes in distinct crystal forms

48. Petrology is a branch of geology concerned with the study of   48._____

    A. oil and gas   B. landforms
    C. rocks   D. fossils

49. A rock structure formed by fracturing of the rock in response to tensional forces is   49._____

    A. foliation   B. columnar structure
    C. slaty cleavage   D. flow structure

50. Rocks are said to be metamorphosed if they were   50._____

    A. recrystallized without melting
    B. compacted by the weight of overlying sediments
    C. cemented by crystallization in the pore spaces
    D. crystallized after melting

KEY (CORRECT ANSWERS)

1.	A	11.	C	21.	C	31.	D	41.	B
2.	C	12.	C	22.	C	32.	C	42.	C
3.	A	13.	D	23.	C	33.	C	43.	A
4.	B	14.	D	24.	C	34.	C	44.	B
5.	D	15.	D	25.	C	35.	C	45.	B
6.	C	16.	C	26.	C	36.	C	46.	A
7.	C	17.	B	27.	B	37.	D	47.	C
8.	D	18.	B	28.	C	38.	A	48.	C
9.	A	19.	A	29.	C	39.	D	49.	B
10.	C	20.	C	30.	B	40.	C	50.	A

TEST 3

Each question or incomplete statement is followed by several suggested answers or completions. Select the one that *BEST* answers the question or completes the statement. *PRINT THE LETTER OF THE CORRECT ANSWER IN THE SPACE AT THE RIGHT.*

1. Coarse, crystalline textures are characteristic of igneous rocks which are   1._____

    A. formed by intrusion
    B. formed by extrusion
    C. light-colored and relatively light-weight
    D. dark-colored and relatively heavy

2. Of the following, the one mineral of hardness 3 that possesses three perfect directions of cleavage is   2._____

    A. gypsum   B. fluorite   C. calcite   D. galena

3. Rhyolite is an extrusive igneous rock which has essentially the same mineral composition as   3._____

    A. gabbro   B. syenite   C. granite   D. diorite

4. The contact between the Newark Series and the New York City Series of rocks is a(n)   4._____

    A. normal fault
    B. conformable sedimentary contact
    C. reverse fault
    D. unconformable sedimentary contact

5. "The present is a key to the past" is a concise statement summarizing the operation of the Law or Doctrine of   5._____

    A. Evolution   B. Uniformitarianism
    C. Neptunism   D. Catastrophism

6. "The Age of Mammals" refers to the   6._____

    A. Mesozoic   B. Cenozoic
    C. Cretaceous   D. Triassic

7. William Smith (1769-1839) made his greatest contributions to the budding science of geology in a field of study which would now be called   7._____

    A. paleontology   B. stratigraphy
    C. petrology   D. geophysics

8. The physiographic province that includes the *MAJOR* part of New York State is the   8._____

    A. Laurentian Uplands   B. Atlantic Coastal Plains
    C. New England Province   D. Appalachian Plateau

9. The temperature of the earth's core is, in degrees C., approximately,   9._____

    A. 1000   B. 2500   C. 25,000   D. 100,000

10. The main geologic activity of young rivers is   10._____

    A. deposition   B. side cutting
    C. down cutting   D. widening its flood plain

11. An alluvial fan may be produced by   11._____

    A. an increase in stream velocity
    B. stream piracy
    C. stream rejuvenation
    D. a reduction in stream velocity

12. When a stream cuts below the water table, it becomes   12._____

    A. graded   B. mature   C. permanent   D. subsequent

13. The number of times northern United States was covered by glacial ice sheets in the Pleistocene Epoch is   13._____

    A. 2   B. 3   C. 4   D. 6

14. The cause of the most recent glacial period in the earth's history is   14._____

    A. not yet established
    B. fluctuation in sunspot activity
    C. variation in inclination of the earth's axis
    D. change in elevation of large surface areas

15. The minimum number of glaciers necessary to form a matter-horn peak is   15._____

    A. 1   B. 2   C. 3   D. 4

16. Kettle holes are *MOST CLOSELY* associated with   16._____

    A. uplift of the land   B. limestone layers
    C. water falls   D. glaciation

17. Which one of the following quadrangles would be *BEST* for presenting a unit on terminal moraines?   17._____

    A. Boothbay, Maine   B. Moses Lake, Washington
    C. Whitewater, Wisconsin   D. Charleston, West Virginia

18. The average depth of the oceans is closest to   18._____

    A. 100 feet   B. 1 mile   C. 2 1/2 miles   D. 10 miles

19. Shorelines which were initially formed by uplift of the coast may be found in   19._____

    A. Florida   B. Bermuda   C. Hawaii   D. Maine

20. A type of sandbar connecting an island to the mainland is called a   20._____

    A. bay mouth bar   B. spit
    C. tombolo   D. headland beach

21. Karst regions are associated with bedrock composed of   21._____

    A. limestone   B. sandstone   C. shales   D. basalt

22. A flat-topped submarine volcanic cone is known as a   22._____

    A. guyot   B. inselberg   C. nappe   D. tombolo

23. How many seconds long is the period of a wave that is 80 feet long traveling at 20 feet   23._____
    per second?

    A. 4   B. 20   C. 60   D. 80

24. Which one of the following would be the most difficult to direct students to find evidences   24._____
    of in New York City?

    A. Fossils   B. Striae   C. Potholes   D. Meanders

25. The river valleys of New York City have as their bedrock   25._____

    A. sandstone   B. limestone   C. gneiss   D. shale

26. The largest figure for the age of the solar system is obtained from the study of   26._____

    A. pre-cambrian rocks   B. Canadian Shield
    C. meteorites   D. Colorado Plateau

27. During which one of the following eras were the rocks of the Adirondack Mountains   27._____
    formed?

    A. Cenozoic   B. Mesozoic
    C. Paleozoic   D. Pre-Cambrian

28. In which one of the following types of rock is quartz *NOT* found?   28._____

    A. Basalt   B. Sandstone
    C. Pegmatite   D. Granite

29. A mineral that has a needle-like structure would be described as   29._____

    A. micaceous   B. columnar
    C. acicular   D. pisolitic

30. The products resulting from the chemical weathering of orthoclase are in which one of   30._____
    the following groups?

    A. Sodium carbonate and potassium hydroxide
    B. Sodium chloride and silica
    C. Potassium carbonate, silica, and clay
    D. potassium carbonate and sodium silicate

31. A mixture in which one atom takes the place of another without changing the form of   31._____
    crystal is termed

    A. isomorphous   B. amorphous
    C. isentropic   D. non-crystalline

32. "Ceiling" height is determined by all *EXCEPT*   32._____

    A. pibal   B. ceiling balloon
    C. searchlight   D. sonar

33. Which one of the following statements about the Van Allen belts is *NOT* true?   33.____

    A. They are belts of radiation.
    B. They form concentric spheres around the earth.
    C. They consist of electrically charged particles.
    D. They are 800 to 40,000 miles thick.

34. Which one of the following statements about the ionosphere is *NOT* true?   34.____

    A. It is known as the Heaviside layer after its discoverer.
    B. It consists of at least three distinct layers.
    C. It reflects all radio waves.
    D. It consists of ions produced by solar radiation.

35. Which one of the satellites below is *NOT* used for communications?   35.____

    A. Echo   B. Telstar   C. Syncom   D. Vanguard

36. The basis for the common road warning "Caution - Bridge freezes before road", is which one of the following?   36.____

    A. The freezing point of steel is below that of concrete.
    B. The bridge is cooled from both top and bottom.
    C. Steel is a better conductor of heat than concrete.
    D. Steel is smoother than concrete.

37. Of the following, which one is the *BEST* explanation for the dark appearance of a tornado?   37.____

    A. Refraction of light by the violent winds
    B. Debris sucked up into the vortex
    C. Water churned by violent winds
    D. Anomalous electrical effects

38. The average thickness of snow, in inches, which is equivalent to one inch of rain is   38.____

    A. 1   B. 5   C. 10   D. 15

39. Under which one of the following conditions will dew form most rapidly? When   39.____

    A. the air is dry and still
    B. a strong wind is blowing
    C. the air is warm and still
    D. still warm air is cooled rapidly

40. Which one of the following is *NOT* necessarily true of a cTw air mass?   40.____

    A. It is relatively uniform
    B. Its origin is continental
    C. Its origin is tropical
    D. It is warm

41. Which type of precipitation below is indicated on weather maps by three horizontal lines?   41.____

    A. Rain   B. Sleet   C. Snow   D. Fog

42. Which one of the following would *NOT* tend to make temperature changes in rising air adiabatic?   42.____

    A. Air is a poor conductor of heat
    B. Air is a poor absorber of heat
    C. Surface air mixes with adjacent air
    D. Expansion occurs as a result of reduced pressure

43. Which one of the following is *NOT* a temperature scale?   43.____

    A. Baumé   B. Celsius   C. Réamur   D. Rankine

44. To which one of the following latitudes are the vertical noontime rays of the sun closest on September 20?   44.____

    A. $0°$ B. $10°\,N$ C. $10°\,S$ D. $23°\,S$

45. The number of degrees of earth latitude over which the noontime vertical rays of the sun travel in a six-month period is closest to   45.____

    A. $23\ 1/2°$ B. $47°$ C. $66\ 1/2°$ D. $90°$

46. The percent of the area of India which is south of the Equator is   46.____

    A. 0%   B. 25%   C. 50%   D. 75%

47. At which one of the following meridians is Mountain Standard Time the standard time?   47.____

    A. $75°\,W$ B. $90°\,W$ C. $105°\,W$ D. $120°\,W$

48. Which one of the following changes is made when a westbound ship crosses the International Date Line at 12 noon on a Wednesday?   48.____

    A. Clocks are moved to 12 midnight on Wednesday
    B. Clocks are moved to 11 A. Wednesday
    C. Calendars are changed to Tuesday
    D. Calendars are changed to Thursday

49. Contour maps do *NOT* show   49.____

    A. latitude and longitude
    B. dip and strike
    C. distance between points on a map
    D. direction in which streams flow

50. Which representative fraction below is closest in equivalence to a scale of 1" per mile?   50.____

    A. 1:31,680   B. 1:62,500
    C. 1:63,360   D. 1:100000

KEY (CORRECT ANSWERS)

1.	A	11.	D	21.	A	31.	A	41.	D
2.	C	12.	C	22.	A	32.	D	42.	C
3.	C	13.	C	23.	A	33.	B	43.	A
4.	D	14.	A	24.	A	34.	C	44.	A
5.	B	15.	C	25.	B	35.	D	45.	B
6.	B	16.	D	26.	C	36.	B	46.	A
7.	B	17.	C	27.	D	37.	B	47.	C
8.	D	18.	C	28.	A	38.	C	48.	D
9.	B	19.	A	29.	C	39.	D	49.	B
10.	C	20.	C	30.	C	40.	D	50.	C

TEST 4

DIRECTIONS: Each question or incomplete statement is followed by several suggested answers or completions. Select the one that *BEST* answers the question or completes the statement. *PRINT THE LETTER OF THE CORRECT ANSWER IN THE SPACE AT THE RIGHT.*

1. As far as we now know, for which one of the reasons below is our moon different from other moons in our solar system?

    A. It is the largest
    B. It is the closest in size to its planet
    C. Its density is almost exactly that of its planet
    D. It is the only one with no atmosphere

1.____

2. Which instrument below is used to photograph stars by the light of a single spectral line?

    A. Coronagraph   B. Pyroheliometer
    C. Spectroheliograph   D. Sun camera

2.____

3. Which one of the constellations below is always visible on clear nights from New York City?

    A. Ursa Major   B. Ursa Minor
    C. Orion   D. Andromeda

3.____

4. Which one of the following is *NOT* a first magnitude star?

    A. Arcturus   B. Capella   C. Rigel   D. Polaris

4.____

5. How many times brighter is a first magnitude star than a third magnitude star?

    A. 2.5   B. 6.3   C. 16   D. 40

5.____

6. Which one of the major planets below has an average density less than that of water?

    A. Jupiter   B. Saturn   C. Uranus   D. Neptune

6.____

7. When the moon is in new crescent phase, in which phase will an astronaut on the moon see the earth?

    A. Full   B. New   C. Crescent   D. Gibbous

7.____

8. In which one of the following ways does the appearance of a star change when viewed with good quality telescopes of higher and higher power?

    A. Apparent size remains constant, brightness increases
    B. Apparent size increases, brightness increases
    C. Color fringes appear
    D. Twinkling decreases

8.____

9. Which feature below is *NOT* part of the solar surface?

    A. Granule   B. Corona
    C. Prominance   D. Bailey's Beads

9.____

10. Which one of the following is used to regulate the buoyancy in the Piccard bathyscaphe?   10.____

    A. Air   B. Helium
    C. Polyurethane foam   D. Gasoline

11. Which one of the following ocean currents flows generally southward?   11.____

    A. Bahama   B. Gulf Stream
    C. Alaska   D. California

12. Of the following, which condition will **prevent the growth of coral reefs**?   12.____

    A. Water temperature below 60° F
    B. Salinity less than 30 parts per thousand
    C. Water depth greater than 50 feet
    D. Lack of adequate sunlight

13. Which one of the following types of shoreline is the result of submergence?   13.____

    A. Fiord   B. Coastal plain
    C. Outwash plain   D. Volcanic island

14. An entrenched meander in the bed of a river indicates   14.____

    A. deepening by valley glaciers
    B. uplift of the region
    C. a limestone bedrock
    D. stream piracy

15. Stream capture may result in the formation of   15.____

    A. water gap   B. wind gap
    C. hanging valley   D. incised meander

16. Of the following, the river that marks a portion of the southern limit of glaciers in North America during the most recent Ice Age is the   16.____

    A. Missouri   B. St. Lawrence
    C. Delaware   D. Hackensack

17. Downfolds of sedimentary rock are called   17.____

    A. anticlines   B. geodynes
    C. isoclines   D. synclines

18. The Badlands of South Dakota have been produced *PRIMARILY* by   18.____

    A. stream erosion   B. wind erosion
    C. glaciation   D. vulcanism

19. Disturbed rock layers are usually associated with   19.____

    A. lacustrine plains   B. coastal plains
    C. flood plains   D. peneplanes

20. Which one of the following is a geologic feature *NOT* characteristic of a glaciated region? A(n)   20.____

    A. kame   B. esker   C. stack   D. drumlin

21. Dreikanters are produced by   21.____

    A. wave erosion   B. wind erosion
    C. glaciers   D. stream erosion

22. An outstanding feature of the Yosemite Valley in California is   22.____

    A. hanging valleys   B. natural bridges
    C. volcanic necks   D. crater lakes

23. Of the following, the one which is a deposit formed by wind is a(n)   23.____

    A. esker   B. barchan   C. spit   D. delta

24. Geodes are formed by   24.____

    A. volcanic action   B. metamorphosis
    C. deposition of minerals   D. meteorites

25. Of the following, the one which is a mineral with no natural cleavage planes is   25.____

    A. mica   B. calcite   C. feldspar   D. quartz

26. The texture of an igneous rock containing large crystals set in a background of small   26.____
    crystals of the same material is

    A. porphyritic   B. granular
    C. glassy   D. aphanitic

27. Fossils are *LEAST* likely to be found in   27.____

    A. sandstone   B. coquina   C. limestone   D. gneiss

28. Galena crystals have which one of the following structures?   28.____

    A. Monoclinic   B. Cubic
    C. Hexagonal   D. Orthorhombic

29. Granite always contains silica and which one of the following?   29.____

    A. Plagioclase feldspar   B. Orthoclase feldspar
    C. Olivine   D. Biotite mica

30. When feldspar decomposes it forms the mineral,   30.____

    A. quartz   B. talc   C. mica   D. kaolinite

31. Old mountains are characterized by   31.____

    A. steep slopes
    B. irregular skyline
    C. extensive earthquake activity
    D. monadnocks

32. A typical artesian formation would be characterized by a   32.____

    A. layer of clay between two layers of granite
    B. layer of quartzite between two layers of clay
    C. layer of sandstone between two layers of shale
    D. surface layer of sand resting on a layer of shale

33. Compared to granite, basalt is *USUALLY*   33.____

  A. lighter in color and less dense
  B. darker in color and less dense
  C. lighter in color and more dense
  D. darker in color and more dense

34. The minimum number of seismograph stations needed to locate the focus of an earth-   34.____
    quake is

  A. one   B. two   C. three   D. four

35. In which one of the following are seismic waves arranged in order of speed, from slowest   35.____
    to fastest?

  A. Long, primary and secondary
  B. Primary, secondary and long
  C. Long, secondary and primary
  D. Secondary, primary and long

36. Tectonic earthquakes are the result of   36.____

  A. crustal movements   B. volcanic activity
  C. tsunamis   D. landslides

37. As far as is now known, the greatest depth of the Earth's oceans, in feet, is closest to   37.____

  A. 10,000   B. 22,000   C. 35,000   D. 60,000

38. The geologic period for which the trilobite is an index fossil is the   38.____

  A. Cambrian   B. Jurassic
  C. Cretaceous   D. Triassic

39. The basin of Crater Lake, Oregon, is a   39.____

  A. sinkhole   B. glacial valley
  C. inland sea   D. caldera

40. Active volcanoes are usually found in areas that include   40.____

  A. dissected plateaus   B. peneplanes
  C. young mountains   D. lacustrine plains

41. The coal deposits in Pennsylvania were formed during which one of the following eras?   41.____

  A. Cenozoic   B. Pre-Cambrian
  C. Paleozoic   D. Mesozoic

42. Which one of the following is *NOT* a silicate mineral?   42.____

  A. Augite   B. Biotite
  C. Olivine   D. Sphalerite

43. The formula for siderite is   43.____

  A. $FeCO_3$ B. $Fe_2O_3 \cdot H_2O$ C. FeS_2 D. Fe_3O_4

44. Of the following chemicals, the one that can be used to simulate the appearance of an erupting volcano is   44.____

    A. potassium chlorate   B. potassium nitrate
    C. ammonium chloride   D. ammonium dichromate

45. The oldest bedrock of New York City is   45.____

    A. dolomite   B. limestone
    C. Manhattan schist   D. Fordham gneiss

46. Carbonado is a gray to black opaque variety of   46.____

    A. graphite   B. lignite
    C. bone fossil   D. diamond

47. Hydrated calcium sulfate is known as   47.____

    A. iceland spar   B. talc   C. calcite   D. gypsum

48. Of the following physical properties, which one is most useful in distinguishing between hematite and limonite?   48.____

    A. Luster   B. Streak   C. Hardness   D. Cleavage

49. Which one of the following is a sedimentary rock?   49.____

    A. Diorite   B. Dolomite   C. Rhyolite   D. Slate

50. Fire Island and Jones Beach are good examples of   50.____

    A. off shore bars   B. barrier reefs
    C. wave built terraces   D. outwash plains

KEY (CORRECT ANSWERS)

1. B	11. D	21. B	31. D	41. C
2. C	12. D	22. A	32. C	42. D
3. B	13. A	23. B	33. D	43. A
4. D	14. B	24. C	34. C	44. D
5. C	15. B	25. D	35. C	45. D
6. B	16. A	26. A	36. A	46. D
7. D	17. D	27. D	37. C	47. D
8. A	18. A	28. B	38. A	48. B
9. D	19. D	29. B	39. D	49. B
10. D	20. C	30. D	40. C	50. A

EXAMINATION SECTION
TEST 1

DIRECTIONS: Each question or incomplete statement is followed by several suggested answers or completions. Select the one that *BEST* answers the question or completes the statement. *PRINT THE LETTER OF THE CORRECT ANSWER IN THE SPACE AT THE RIGHT.*

1. Of the following, it is correct to say that as colder ocean water sinks to the ocean bottom it has a tendency to "creep"   1._____

    A.   toward the equator
    B.   toward the North and South Poles
    C.   eastward
    D.   westward

2. Of the following, the one that is *NOT* a factor contributing to the origin and distribution of ocean currents is the   2._____

    A.   prevailing winds   B.   changing tides
    C.   rotation of the earth   D.   shape of continents

3. Coral reefs have the best chance of becoming established in warm shallow waters where   3._____

    A.   waves and currents are active
    B.   there is little or no motion
    C.   rocks on which they form are frequently exposed to air
    D.   turbidity is great

4. Of the following, it is correct to say that, if coral grows upward as fast as an island sinks, the reef will   4._____

    A.   come closer to the sinking land
    B.   get farther from the sinking land
    C.   not change its size
    D.   grow equally both toward the island and seaward

5. Of the following locations, submarine canyons extending across a continental shelf may occur where   5._____

    A.   rivers enter the ocean
    B.   littoral currents are especially strong
    C.   fault lines extend out from the coast
    D.   tidal forces are unusual

6. A tombolo is a variety of   6._____

    A.   concretion   B.   lake   C.   sand bar   D.   volcano

7. The Humboldt current is located in the   7._____

    A.   south pacific   B.   north pacific
    C.   south atlantic   D.   north atlantic

8. Where two valley glaciers come together, deposition may result in the formation of   8.____

    A. terminal moraine   B. esker
    C. lateral moraine   D. medial moraine

9. Of the following forms of ice, which one had a terrestrial origin although it is found in sea   9.____
waters?

    A. Pack ice   B. Ice floes   C. Icebergs   D. Ice foot

10. Of the following evidences, which one does NOT indicate the general direction of move-   10.____
ment of a glacier?

    A. Striae
    B. Direction of flow of post-glacial streams
    C. Roche moutonnees
    D. U-shaped valleys

11. The total relief of the earth is closest, in miles, to which one of the following?   11.____

    A. 5   B. 7   C. 12   D. 17

12. Of the following, the rock most rapidly eroded by ground water is   12.____

    A. breccia   B. sandstone   C. shale   D. limestone

13. Elongated ridges of till, usually in clusters, and oval in shape are known as   13.____

    A. kames   B. eskers   C. drumlins   D. outliers

14. Of the following, a mineral that will effervesce with warm dilute hydrochloric acid is   14.____

    A. selenite   B. dolomite   C. fluorite   D. biotite

15. The "moho" refers to   15.____

    A. a deep in the Pacific Ocean
    B. the boundary between the crust and the mantle
    C. a type of drilling machine
    D. a fault in the crust of the earth

16. Of the following, the drainage pattern typical of a dome mountain region is   16.____

    A. dendritic   B. radial and annular
    C. rectangular   D. trellis

17. Of the following, the agent of erosion that produces ventifacts is the   17.____

    A. driving force of wind blown sand
    B. milling action of sub-glacial streams
    C. chemical action of ground water
    D. pounding force of waves

18. To be of most use to the geologist, the organism in an index fossil should have existed   18.____
over a

    A. widespread area for a relatively short period of time
    B. widespread area for a relatively long period of time

C. relatively narrow range of area for a short period of time
D. relatively narrow range of area for a long period of time

19. Of the following, the earliest event in the development of a folded mountain range is   19.____

A. folding and metamorphism of sediments
B. formation of a geosyncline
C. extrusive and intrusive volcanic activity
D. deposition of sediments

20. The divide between two stream systems shifts in the direction of the system   20.____

A. having the steeper gradients
B. having the gentler gradients
C. eroding more resistant rocks
D. receiving the greater volume of precipitation

21. The concept of isostasy has been used to explain the   21.____

A. original formation of continents and ocean basins
B. occurrence of earthquakes and volcanic activity along the shores of the Pacific Ocean
C. origin of flat-topped submarine mountains in the Pacific Ocean
D. alternation of glacial and inter-glacial stages in the Pleistocene epoch

22. When a river that is in its old age stage is rejuvenated, which one of the following is most likely to form?   22.____

A. Levee   B. Flood plain
C. Intrenched meander   D. Alluvial cone

23. The Cambrian period is characterized by   23.____

A. the advent of man
B. widespread vulcanism
C. the first abundant fossils
D. the first appearance of glaciers

24. Of the following, the Ewing-Donn hypothesis attempts to explain the   24.____

A. origin and development of folded mountains
B. origin and formation of submarine canyons
C. cause and distribution of earthquakes
D. onset and succession of glacial stages in the Northern hemisphere

25. The most recent age determinations of rocks by radioactive methods indicate that the length of geologic time is   25.____

A. approximately 1 1/2 billion years
B. between 2 and 2 1/2 billion years
C. in excess of 3 billion years
D. approximately 5 billion years

26. Of the following events which occur in mountain-building, the *LAST* in the sequence is   26.____

    A. lithification of sediments
    B. folding of sedimentary rocks
    C. invasion of roots by magma
    D. elevation of sedimentary rocks

27. Clay varves are useful to geologists in their study of   27.____

    A. climates of the past   B. fossils
    C. ripple marks   D. weathering

28. Of the following, the measurement of the interfacial angles of a crystal is accomplished   28.____
by the use of the instrument known as a

    A. spectrometer   B. clinometer
    C. goniometer   D. refractometer

29. Of the following, the most likely source of heat energy necessary to keep magna in a   29.____
molten condition is

    A. residual heat within the earth's crust
    B. bombardment of the earth by cosmic rays
    C. energy released by radio-active disintegration within the earth's crust
    D. infra-red radiation from the sun

30. Guyots are   30.____

    A. steep-cliff mountains
    B. deep-sea trenches
    C. flat-topped mountains rising from the sea floor
    D. submarine valleys

31. The most recent of the following processes responsible for the hilly topography of north-   31.____
ern Manhattan and the Bronx is

    A. synclinal folding   B. anticlinal folding
    C. volcanic intrusions   D. differential erosion

32. Of the following, the concept of magmatic differentiation is useful in explaining the   32.____

    A. diversity of composition of igneous rocks
    B. difference between intrusive and extrusive igneous rocks
    C. difference between the various phases of volcanic activity
    D. diversity of igneous structures

33. In the history of mountain formation from isostatic readjustment, the first step would be   33.____

    A. formation of a geosyncline
    B. synclinal folding
    C. anticlinal folding
    D. vulcanism

34. A cyclothem is a repetitive series of sedimentary rocks deposited under the condition of alternating cycles of   34._____

    A. glacial and interglacial deposition
    B. dry and wet climatic intervals
    C. marine transgression and regression
    D. fresh water and salt water inudation

35. Phyllite is formed by metamorphism of   35._____

    A. sandstone   B. shale   C. limestone   D. granite

36. Most of the surface bedrock of New York State was formed from sand, mud or limestone deposited in seas and lakes during which one of the following eras?   36._____

    A. Cenozoic   B. Mesozoic
    C. Paleozoic   D. Proterozoic

37. The magma which erupts as extensive basaltic lava flows, probably originates in   37._____

    A. sialic crust   B. simatic crust
    C. earth's mantle   D. earth's core

38. Columnar jointing, a characteristic of igneous rocks, is the result of   38._____

    A. expansion due to heating
    B. contraction due to cooling
    C. contact metamorphism
    D. mineral displacement

39. The white bands in gneiss consist principally of which one of the following pairs?   39._____

    A. Quartz and muscovite   B. Biotite and feldspar
    C. Quartz and feldspar   D. Biotite and amphiboles

40. Calcite deposits around mineral springs are called   40._____

    A. gypsum   B. onyx   C. sphalerite   D. travertine

41. Of the following, a physical property common to granite, basalt and obsidian is   41._____

    A. overall hardness greater than 5
    B. predominantly dark color
    C. specific gravity of 2.7 or less
    D. uniform size of the mineral grains

42. Of the following, a rock which *CANNOT* be classified on the basis of its mineral content is   42._____

    A. basalt   B. shale   C. obsidian   D. marble

43. Our best estimate of the age of the earth is derived from   43._____

    A. the amount of salt in the sea
    B. the study of erosion
    C. the total thickness of sedimentary rock layers
    D. radioactive decay products in rocks

44. Of the following, the one which represents a sequence of increasing metamorphism in rock formation is

    A. shale, phyllite, slate, schist
    B. shale, slate, phyllite, schist
    C. shale, schist, slate, phyllite
    D. shale, slate, schist, phyllite

44.____

45. On the Mohs' scale of hardness, quartz is closest to which one of the following?

    A. 2   B. 4   C. 7   D. 9

45.____

46. Which one of the following *BEST* describes the mineral composition of a granite?

    A. Biotite, orthoclase, quartz
    B. Quartz, calcite, talc
    C. Mica, hornblende, olivine
    D. Calcite, feldspar, magnetite

46.____

47. Of the following, the type of cloud most likely to produce a halo around the moon is

    A. cumulonimbus   B. altocumulus
    C. cirrocumulus   D. cirrostratus

47.____

48. The wave length of an ocean wave represents the distance from the

    A. crest of one wave to the trough of the next wave
    B. crest of wave to the trough of the same wave
    C. trough of one wave to the trough of the next wave
    D. crest of one wave to the crest of the next wave divided by 2

48.____

49. A great deal of seaweed accumulates in the Sargasso Sea largely because

    A. of warm Equatorial air
    B. of unusual quantities of sunshine
    C. there is little current in the central part of an ocean
    D. in that area there are too few fish to consume the plants

49.____

50. If iron were left on the surface of the moon, it would probably

    A. remain chemically unchanged
    B. change to Fe_2O_3 more quickly than on earth
    C. change to FeS
    D. change to Fe_2O_3 at a rate approximately 1/7 of the rate of iron's corrosion on earth

50.____

KEY (CORRECT ANSWERS)

1.	A	11.	C	21.	B	31.	D	41.	A
2.	B	12.	D	22.	C	32.	A	42.	C
3.	A	13.	C	23.	C	33.	A	43.	D
4.	B	14.	B	24.	D	34.	C	44.	B
5.	A	15.	B	25.	C	35.	B	45.	C
6.	C	16.	B	26.	D	36.	C	46.	A
7.	A	17.	A	27.	A	37.	B	47.	D
8.	D	18.	A	28.	C	38.	B	48.	C
9.	C	19.	B	29.	C	39.	C	49.	C
10.	B	20.	B	30.	C	40.	D	50.	A

TEST 2

DIRECTIONS: Each question or incomplete statement is followed by several suggested answers or completions. Select the one that *BEST* answers the question or completes the statement. *PRINT THE LETTER OF THE CORRECT ANSWER IN THE SPACE AT THE RIGHT.*

1. Of the following, which rock is the extrusive equivalent of gabbro?   1.____

    A. Andesite   B. Basalt   C. Dacite   D. Rhyolite

2. Relatively quiet bodies of water between offshore bars and the mainland are called   2.____

    A. lagoons   B. fjords   C. shoals   D. tidal races

3. According to most recent scientific estimates based on radioactivity, the earth's age, in years, is closest to which one of the following?   3.____

    A. 40 million   B. 400 million   C. 4 billion   D. 40 billion

4. Calcium carbonate deposited from ground water is called   4.____

    A. geyserite   B. ocher   C. travertine   D. gypsum

5. Which one of the following metals is usually extracted commercially from sea water?   5.____

    A. Iron   B. Aluminum   C. Magnesium   D. Titanium

6. Which one of the following is a mineral that is isomorphic with magnesite?   6.____

    A. Siderite   B. Selenite   C. Albite   D. Biotite

7. The large crystals in a porphyry are called   7.____

    A. aphanites   B. metacrysts   C. phenocrysts   D. porphyrites

8. Dinosaurs were the dominant form of life in which one of the following periods?   8.____

    A. Cambrian   B. Jurassic   C. Permian   D. Carboniferous

9. An obsequent stream would be found   9.____

    A. on the inface of a cuesta
    B. on the backslope of a hogback
    C. in a belt of weak rock parallel to the coastline
    D. in the direction of the consequent streams

10. Of the following, which one is a narrow block of rock uplifted between two normal faults?   10.____

    A. Flatiron   B. Horst   C. Polje   D. Stack

11. Of the following statements concerning bodies of water, the one which is correct is: 11.____

    A. The Caspian Sea is a fresh water lake.
    B. Lake Ronkonkoma is of glacial origin.
    C. Lake Champlain has been a fresh water lake since its formation.
    D. Lake Mead was formed by impounding river water behind the Grand Coulee Dam.

12. The Badlands of South Dakota are cut up by numerous small gullies. These features were formed mainly by   12.____

    A. waves   B. glacial action
    C. winds   D. running water

13. "Chimney rocks" or "stacks" are largely the result of   13.____

    A. wind erosion   B. weathering
    C. glaciation   D. wave erosion

14. Of the following, the mineral which is *NOT* a sulfide is   14.____

    A. chalcocite   B. sphalerite
    C. galena   D. cassiterite

15. Which one of the following is an example of block mountains?   15.____

    A. Sierra Nevadas   B. Black Hills
    C. Andes   D. Appalachians

16. Loess is a result of deposition by   16.____

    A. gravity   B. wind
    C. ground water   D. ocean currents

17. During a long period of drought, deep rooted plants may obtain a limited water supply from immediately above the water table. This water is obtained from ground water and moves upward through the soil because of   17.____

    A. cohesive forces
    B. viscous flow
    C. its seeking its own level
    D. capillary action

18. A barchan is a variety of   18.____

    A. cave   B. concretion   C. monadnock   D. dune

19. Which one of the following is a physiographic feature that requires a rise of land or a fall in sea level for its development?   19.____

    A. Alluvial fan   B. Intrenched meander
    C. Oxbow lake   D. Sea cave

20. In the field of earth science, a pediment may be defined as a(n)   20.____

    A. unattached sand bar at the mouth of a bay
    B. smooth sloping rock surface fringing a desert mountain range
    C. lava flow that has dammed a river to form a lake
    D. monadnock in an old plateau region

21. Of the following rocks, the kind in which fossils are most likely to be found is   21.____

    A. granite   B. basalt   C. pumice   D. sandstone

22. The fractional scale 1:24,000 represents a map scale of 1 inch to   22._____

    A. 1/2 mile   B. 1,200 meters
    C. 800 yards   D. 2,000 feet

23. Of the following, which one is a correct description of the Catskills?   23._____

    A. Complex mountains   B. Domed mountains
    C. Folded mountains   D. Dissected plateaus

24. The presence of which one of the following causes the red coloring of many rocks and   24._____
soils?

    A. Hematite   B. Sphalerite
    C. Cinnabar   D. Calcite

25. The average speed, in miles per second, of the primary wave set up by an earthquake is   25._____
closest to which one of the following?

    A. 1   B. 5   C. 20   D. 186,000

26. The most recently active volcano in the contiguous 48 states of the continental United   26._____
States area is

    A. Mount Hood   B. Mount Shasta
    C. Mount Lassen   D. Mount Rainier

27. Our most recent continental glacier withdrew from north-central North America at a num-   27._____
ber of years ago closest to

    A. 1,000   B. 9,000   C. 60,000   D. 1,000,000

28. The brightest "star" in the night time sky of either hemisphere is   28._____

    A. Venus   B. Canopus   C. Betelgeuse   D. Sirius

29. Mechanical disintegration due to temperature changes is most pronounced in the United   29._____
States

    A. in arid regions and on exposed mountain summits
    B. in sandy deserts
    C. on northern slopes
    D. in regions of warm temperature and high humidity

30. The vertical displacement of a fault block is known as the   30._____

    A. heave   B. throw   C. dip slope   D. strike slip

31. The auroras are believed to result from   31._____

    A. interaction of earth's magnetic field with particles emitted by the sun
    B. annihilation of electrons and positrons in upper regions of the atmosphere
    C. creation of glowing particles by interaction of cosmic rays
    D. emission of electrical particles from outer galaxies

32. A man-made earth satellite is most likely to collide with a   32._____

    A. comet   B. planet   C. meteor   D. planetoid

33. To which one of the following phenomena is the blue color of the sky attributed? 33.____

    A. Differential scattering
    B. Total internal reflection
    C. Absorption
    D. Refraction

34. Of the following, which one is an effective moderator for an atomic reactor? 34.____

    A. Boron steel
    C. Cadmium
    B. Lead
    D. Heavy water

35. To which one of the following is a Geiger counter most likely to respond? 35.____

    A. Galena
    C. Pitchblende
    B. Limonite
    D. Pyroxene

36. The ratio of the brightness of a star of the first magnitude to that of a star of the second magnitude is 36.____

    A. 2:1   B. 2.5:1   C. 4:1   D. 8:1

37. The "Bad Lands" of South Dakota is an example of which one of the following kinds of sculpture? 37.____

    A. Wind
    C. Glacier
    B. Wave
    D. Stream and rain

38. Topographic maps utilize 38.____

    A. only one contour interval for each map
    B. the changing of a contour interval in abrupt changes from plains areas to very mountainous areas
    C. no definite contour interval
    D. depression contours to indicate submarine depths along shorelines

39. Which one of the following contributed most to the development of the air mass theory of weather? 39.____

    A. Ferrel
    C. Petterssen
    B. Guys-Ballot
    D. Bergeron

40. The man named below most likely to be associated with the Cosmogonists is 40.____

    A. William Smith
    C. René Descartes
    B. Seneca
    D. Cuvier

41. The Polar-front theory to explain the origin of cyclones and anticyclones originated with 41.____

    A. Brunt   B. Shaw   C. Murphy   D. Bjerknes

42. The igneous activity which produced the rock of the Palisades of the Hudson River occurred principally during the geologic period called 42.____

    A. Triassic
    C. Cretaceous
    B. Jurassic
    D. Eocene

43. It is not possible to correlate reliably Precambrian rocks between different regions of the continent because of the

    A. intense deformation
    B. lack of uranium ores
    C. absence of fossils
    D. lack of sedimentary deposits

43.____

44. In which one of the geologic eras were the rocks of Manhattan and the Bronx formed?

    A. Archeozoic
    C. Mesozoic
    B. Proterozoic
    D. Cenozoic

44.____

45. Which one of the following actions is a factor in the formation of the basins of karst lakes?

    A. Landslide
    C. Volcanic
    B. Glacial
    D. Ground water

45.____

46. Which one of the following is *NOT* associated with unconsolidated material when it is attacked by waves?

    A. Wave-cut terrace
    C. Wave-cut cliff
    B. Wave-built terrace
    D. Wave-cut notch

46.____

47. Of the following, which one is *NOT* associated with rock phenomena originating from ground water?

    A. Geodes
    C. Petrified wood
    B. Travertine
    D. Arêtes

47.____

48. Great Salt Lake, together with which one of the following, constitutes much of the area once filled by ancient Lake Bonneville?

    A. Lake Sevier
    C. Lake Winnipeg
    B. Death Valley
    D. Salton Sea

48.____

49. Which one of the following bodies of water has no outlet?

    A. Lake Superior
    C. Lake Cayuga
    B. Caspian Sea
    D. Lake Huron

49.____

50. According to Gilbert's sixth power law, if the velocity of a stream is doubled, the size of the particles composing the load may be increased up to how many times?

    A. 12   B. 24   C. 32   D. 64

50.____

KEY (CORRECT ANSWERS)

1.	B	11.	B	21.	D	31.	A	41.	D
2.	A	12.	D	22.	D	32.	C	42.	A
3.	C	13.	D	23.	D	33.	A	43.	C
4.	C	14.	D	24.	A	34.	D	44.	A
5.	C	15.	A	25.	B	35.	C	45.	D
6.	A	16.	B	26.	C	36.	B	46.	C
7.	C	17.	D	27.	B	37.	D	47.	D
8.	B	18.	D	28.	D	38.	B	48.	A
9.	A	19.	B	29.	A	39.	D	49.	B
10.	B	20.	B	30.	B	40.	C	50.	D

TEST 3

Each question or incomplete statement is followed by several suggested answers or completions. Select the one that *BEST* answers the question or completes the statement. *PRINT THE LETTER OF THE CORRECT ANSWER IN THE SPACE AT THE RIGHT.*

1. Which one of the following rocks is known to be most radioactive?

   A. Gabbro   B. Granite   C. Basalt   D. Sandstone

1.____

2. Which one of the following upon being subjected to contact metamorphism may develop into two different rocks?

   A. Conglomerate   B. Sandstone
   C. Shale   D. Limestone

2.____

3. Columnar jointing is associated with the cooling of

   A. diorite   B. syenite   C. diabase   D. granite

3.____

4. Which one of the following is *NOT* a sedimentary rock?

   A. Conglomerate   B. Chert
   C. Sandstone   D. Gabbro

4.____

5. Which one of the following rocks is formed when talus materials are cemented together?

   A. Tuff   B. Breccia
   C. Consolidated gravel   D. Conglomerate

5.____

6. Residual mantle rock

   A. may be found below a mantle of transported rock
   B. is never found below a mantle rock
   C. is found in desert areas only
   D. does not resemble the bedrock below it

6.____

7. Which one of the following rocks is classified as metamorphic?

   A. Syenite   B. Rhyolite
   C. Quartzite   D. Marl

7.____

8. Which one of the following pairs associates a characteristic of diorite with one of granite?

   A. Little visible quartz and oligoclase feldspar
   B. Large crystals of quartz and plagioclase feldspar
   C. Large crystals of quartz and oligoclase feldspar
   D. Little visible quartz and a predominance of plagioclase feldspar

8.____

9. Which one of the following is *NOT* an intrusive igneous rock?

   A. Stocks   B. Tufa bed
   C. Laccoliths   D. Batholith

9.____

10. The schistose texture of metamorphic rocks is best described by which one of the following?   10.____

    A. Roughly foliated, alternating parallel bands of light and dark colored minerals
    B. Well foliated, consisting dominantly of mica minerals large enough to be recognized
    C. Foliated, but with no recognizable minerals
    D. Nonfoliated, mineral grains interlocked

11. Which one of the following groups describes orthoclase feldspar?   11.____

    A. 2 cleavage planes meeting at right angles, hardness of 6
    B. 2 cleavage planes meeting at $56°$ and $124°$ angles, hardness of 5 to 6
    C. 3 cleavage planes not at right angles to each other, hardness of 3
    D. No cleavage planes, hardness of 7

12. Which one of the following is the formula for magnetite?   12.____

    A. Fe_2O_3 B. Fe_3O_4
    C. $Fe_2O_3 \cdot H_2O$ D. $Fe_2O_3 \cdot 3H_2O$

13. Which one of the following minerals is used as an electrical insulator?   13.____

    A. Muscovite   B. Chlorite
    C. Plagioclase   D. Albite

14. In which one of the following forms are the atoms in a diamond arranged?   14.____

    A. Rings of six   B. A cube
    C. A rhomboid   D. A tetrahedron

15. Which one of the following pairs characterizes halite?   15.____

    A. Colorless, hardness of 2.5
    B. Purple color, hardness of 4
    C. Lead gray, hardness of 2.5
    D. Brassy yellow color, hardness of 6

16. Few surface streams are found in Yucatan because the underlying rock is   16.____

    A. sandstone   B. limestone
    C. conglomerate   D. shale

17. Deep, black color in limestone cave deposits indicates the presence of   17.____

    A. ferric oxide   B. manganese dioxide
    C. carbon   D. graphite

18. Which one of the following minerals exhibits the nearly perfect cleavage?   18.____

    A. Mica   B. Gypsum   C. Calcite   D. Feldspar

19. To which one of the following crystal systems does garnet belong?   19.____

    A. Tetragonal   B. Isometric
    C. Triclinic   D. Hexagonal

20. The coalescence of several high mountain glaciers results in the formation of a(n)   20._____

    A. cirque   B. esker
    C. piedmont glacier   D. plateau glacier

21. Werner's Theory stated that   21._____

    A. basalt originated by volcanic action
    B. all rocks of the earth were precipitated from a universal ocean
    C. dense, fine-grained basalt was associated with scoria
    D. fused basalt produces a glassy rock

22. If the hanging wall in a fault has been forced upward relative to the foot wall, the resulting   22._____
formation is described as which one of the following faults?

    A. normal   B. reverse   C. horizontal   D. tensional

23. When an upthrown block of the earth's crust is bounded on two sides by faults, it is called   23._____
a(n)

    A. graben   B. overthrust block
    C. lateral thrust block   D. horst

24. Which one of the following terms is *NOT* associated with the concept of weathering?   24._____

    A. Frost heaving   B. Growing roots of trees
    C. Burrowing rodents   D. Mass wasting

25. The dry adiabatic lapse rate is *CLOSEST* to which one of the following?   25._____

    A. $1.5°$ F per 1000 feet   B. $5.5°$ F per 1000 feet
    C. $6.5°$ F per 500 feet   D. $9.5°$ F per 500 feet

26. Felsenmeer result primarily from   26._____

    A. frost action   B. wind erosion
    C. faulting   D. carbonation

27. The chemical weathering of orthoclase may result in the formation of which one of the   27._____
following groups?

    A. Clay, carbon dioxide, potassium sulfate
    B. Clay, silica, potassium carbonate
    C. Bauxite, limonite and carbon dioxide
    D. Calcium bicarbonate, silica, potassium carbonate

28. Which one of the following conditions will favor the growth of coral?   28._____

    A. Salt water, 240 ft. deep at $58°$
    B. Salt water, 120 ft. deep at $68°$ F
    C. Salt water, 120 ft. deep at $58°$ F
    D. Fresh water, 120 ft. deep at $68°$ F

29. Which one of the following combinations will produce the highest tides? 29.____

    A. Moon at apogee, sun at perihelion, low barometric pressure, wind with the tide
    B. Moon at perigee, sun at perihelion, high barometric pressure, wind with the tide
    C. Moon at perigee, sun at perihelion, high barometric pressure, wind against the tide
    D. Moon at perigee, sun at perihelion, low barometric pressure, wind with the tide

30. Tsunamis are *MOST CLOSELY* associated with 30.____

    A. meteorological disturbance
    B. seismological disturbance
    C. solar gravitational attraction
    D. lunar gravitational attraction

31. Of which one of the following shorelines is the Chesapeake Bay region an example? 31.____

    A. Neutral   B. Ria   C. Fiord   D. Delta

32. If it is high tide at 3:00 p.m., the next high tide will occur at a time *CLOSEST* to which one of the following? 32.____

    A. 3:52 p.m.   B. 9:13 p.m.
    C. 3:26 a.m.   D. 9:13 a.m.

33. According to the theory of isostasy, the bedrock of the oceanic basins consists essentially of 33.____

    A. sandstone   B. basalt   C. granite   D. limestone

34. Which one of the following currents occurs when large waves cause water to pile up on the shore area? 34.____

    A. Tidal   B. Rip   C. Longshore   D. Surf

35. Which one of the following statements is *NOT* a true description of ocean wave phenomena? 35.____

    A. Water particles in waves move along at the same velocity as the wave.
    B. Waves originate by the frictional action of wind on water.
    C. Energy is imparted to waves by winds.
    D. Wave height is the vertical distance between crest and trough.

36. Uparchings many miles wide and hundreds of miles long are known as 36.____

    A. anticlines   B. domes
    C. laccoliths   D. geanticlines

37. Tuff originates from action of 37.____

    A. rivers   B. volcanoes   C. glaciers   D. geysers

38. Which one of the following stages of concentration of carbon is *NOT* represented in the production of hard-coal? 38.____

    A. Lignite   B. Bituminous   C. Peat   D. Graphite

39. With which one of the following groups may the Adirondacks be classified?   39.____

    A. Laurentian Upland, Younger Appalachian, Southern Rockies
    B. Laurentian Upland, New England, Southern Rockies
    C. New England, Older Appalachians, Younger Appalachians
    D. New England, Younger Appalachians, Southern Appalachians

40. In which one of the following states is the largest single block of faulted mountain area   40.____
located?

    A. Utah   B. California   C. Oregon   D. Nevada

41. Which one of the following metamorphic rocks has concretionary lumps through it?   41.____

    A. Schist   B. Banded gneiss
    C. Augen gneiss   D. Foliated gneiss

42. In the principle of superposition it was recognized that   42.____

    A. the bed of sedimentary rock at the lowest level must be the oldest
    B. the bed of sedimentary rock at the lowest level must be the youngest
    C. the beds of sedimentary rocks do not follow an orderly succession toward the top
    D. the correlation of sedimentary rocks can be well utilized

43. Which one of the following minerals is *LEAST* likely to be found in a light colored, course-   43.____
grained granite?

    A. Orthoclase   B. Olivine
    C. Plagioclase   D. Quartz

44. Which one of the following groups does *NOT* consist of plateaus having a common ori-   44.____
gin?

    A. Allegheny, Catskill, Colorado
    B. Cumberland, Allegheny, Catskill
    C. Cumberland, Colorado, Columbia
    D. Cumberland, Colorado, Allegheny

45. Classic examples of breached anticlines and synclines may be found in which one of the   45.____
following physiographic areas?

    A. Cascade Mountains
    B. Adirondack Mountains
    C. Younger Appalachian Mountains
    D. Older Appalachian Mountains

46. Assume that an airplane takes off from New York City (longitude 75° W.) at 10 a.m. East-   46.____
ern Standard Time and heads toward London (longitude 0°). If the flying time is 5 hours,
the London standard time at which the plane will reach its destination is

    A. 2 a.m. the next day   B. 3 p.m. the same day
    C. 8 p.m. the same day   D. 10 p.m. the same day

47. In successful drilling for oil from the surface downward in anticlinical structures, one would probably encounter the indicated three substances in which one of the following orders?

47.____

    A. Oil, water, gas   B. Water, gas, oil
    C. Gas, water, oil   D. Gas, oil, water

48. With which one of the following is a peneplane very closely associated?

48.____

    A. Dried up lake bottom   B. Outwash planes
    C. Monadnocks   D. Young Mountains

49. Which one of the following types of springs will result when the surface of the land intersects the water table?

49.____

    A. Artesian   B. Contact
    C. Tubular   D. Oases and tubular

50. Which one of the following physiographic features is *MOST* characteristic of the north shore of Long Island?

50.____

    A. Karst topography   B. Outwash plains
    C. Terminal moraine   D. Barrier beaches

KEY (CORRECT ANSWERS)

1.	B	11.	A	21.	B	31.	B	41.	C
2.	C	12.	B	22.	B	32.	C	42.	A
3.	C	13.	A	23.	D	33.	B	43.	B
4.	D	14.	D	24.	D	34.	B	44.	C
5.	B	15.	A	25.	B	35.	A	45.	C
6.	A	16.	B	26.	A	36.	D	46.	C
7.	C	17.	B	27.	B	37.	B	47.	D
8.	D	18.	A	28.	B	38.	D	48.	C
9.	B	19.	B	29.	D	39.	B	49.	B
10.	B	20.	C	30.	B	40.	B	50.	C

61

TEST 4

DIRECTIONS: Each question or incomplete statement is followed by several suggested answers or completions. Select the one that *BEST* answers the question or completes the statement. *PRINT THE LETTER OF THE CORRECT ANSWER IN THE SPACE AT THE RIGHT.*

1. When surface air at a temperature of 80° F rises 2000 feet without reaching its dew point, its temperature becomes   1._____

    A.   65° F   B.   69° F   C.   73° F   D.   74.5° F

2. The upper portion of a body of water warms up more slowly than an adjacent sandy beach for all of the following reasons *EXCEPT:*   2._____

    A.   The water surface reflects more sunlight than the sand.
    B.   Water is a poorer absorber of insolation than sand.
    C.   Sunlight penetrates to greater depths in water than into sand.
    D.   The specific heat of water is less than that of sand.

3. A west coast region over which the horse latitudes and the prevailing westerlies alternate would have   3._____

    A.   dry summers and dry winters
    B.   dry summers and rainy winters
    C.   wet summers and dry winters
    D.   wet summers and rainy winters

4. Which one of the following minerals gives a red flame test?   4._____

    A.   Rhodonite   B.   Rhodochrosite
    C.   Celestite   D.   Zincite

5. Which one of the following pairs of elements is found in the mineral gypsum?   5._____

    A.   Magnesium and sodium   B.   Calcium and sulphur
    C.   Calcium and sodium   D.   Magnesium and sulphur

6. Which one of the following minerals can scratch glass?   6._____

    A.   Galena   B.   Fluorite   C.   Dolomite   D.   Pyrite

7. Which one of the following minerals has the *HIGHEST* specific gravity?   7._____

    A.   Garnet   B.   Hornblende
    C.   Barite   D.   Albite

8. Of the following, an example of a mineral with perfect octahedral cleavage is   8._____

    A.   sphalerite   B.   diamond
    C.   magnetite   D.   corundum

9. Of the following, the *MOST IMPORTANT* ore of zinc is   9._____

    A.   hematite   B.   cinnabar
    C.   zincite   D.   sphalerite

10. Sapphire is a gem variety of the mineral,   10._____

    A. beryl   B. kyanite   C. corundum   D. sodalite

11. A feature of sedimentary rocks which can be used to distinguish the top from the bottom   11._____
of beds is a(n)

    A. chalk deposit   B. even lamination
    C. oscillation ripple mark   D. torrential cross bedding

12. The most definite evidence of a continental (subaerial) deposit is the formation of   12._____

    A. torrential cross-bedding
    B. ripple marks
    C. arkose sandstone
    D. graded bedding

13. A young river is characterized by   13._____

    A. natural levees   B. flood plains
    C. slight meandering   D. rapids

14. Which one of the following depressions is most commonly found in a region underlaid   14._____
with limestone?

    A. Deflation hollows   B. Sink holes
    C. Plunge basins   D. Craters

15. When estuaries are restricted to one section of a coast line, it means that there was a   15._____

    A. rise of the coast line
    B. lowering of sea level
    C. subsidence of the coast line
    D. rise of sea level

16. Bronx, New York, lies in the physiographic province known as the   16._____

    A. New England Upland   B. Coastal Plain
    C. Triassic Lowland   D. Piedmont

17. Which one of the following is properly classified as an erosional process?   17._____

    A. Exfoliation on a cliff
    B. Fire spalling
    C. Sand blast action in a desert
    D. Wedgework of ice

18. Annular drainage is characteristic of areas in which the dominant rock structure is   18._____

    A. domed   B. faulted   C. folded   D. isoclinal

19. Barchanes are wind deposits that have   19._____

    A. crescent shapes with steep leeward slopes
    B. crescent shapes with steep windward slopes
    C. crescent shapes with the cusps pointing into the wind
    D. circular shapes with even slopes

20. Which one of the following is NOT an epeiric sea?   20._____
    A. Salton Sea   B. Hudson Bay
    C. White Sea   D. Baltic Sea

21. The topography of northern Long Island is characterized by MANY   21._____

    A. drumlins   B. eskers
    C. knobs and kettles   D. outwash plains

22. In which one of the following national parks is Half Dome, an example of exfoliation,   22._____
    located?
    A. Bryce   B. Yellowstone
    C. Yosemite   D. Zion

23. The type of stream which will form on a newly-uplifted coastal plain is   23._____
    A. consequent   B. subsequent
    C. obsequent   D. antecedent

24. Which one of the following is dominant when a stream is in the stage of maturity?   24._____
    A. Downward erosion   B. Headward erosion
    C. Lateral erosion   D. Hydraulic erosion

25. The Colorado River at the Grand Canyon is an example of a   25._____
    A. young river   B. mature river
    C. late mature river   D. old river

26. It has been concluded that the speed of the "L" (Long)waves of seismic disturbances   26._____
    probably indicates that
    B. continents consist of granite and the ocean basins of basalt
    C. continents consist of basalt and the ocean basins of granite
    D. continents and ocean basins consist of granite
    E. continents and ocean basins consist of granite and basalt

27. As one approaches the pole, the number of miles representing one degree of   27._____
    longitude
    A. increases   C. decreases
    B. remains the same   D. varies irregularly

28. Which one of the following did NOT result from metamorphism?   28._____
    A. Foliation   C. Slaty cleavage
    B. Schistosity   D. Stratification

29. Which one of the following types of metamorphism results from the weight of   29._____
    overlying rock layers?
    A. Contact   C. Dynamic
    B. Kinetic   D. Load

30. Which one of the following map scales corresponds to a scale of 1 inch to the mile?   30._____
    A. 1/5280   B. 1/31680
    C. 1/63,360   D. 1/126,720

31. Which one of the following conditions is a deterrent to the growth of coral polyps?   31._____

    A. Depth of 50 feet
    B. Temperature of 75° F
    C. Salt water currents
    D. Muddy water

32. On the average, the continental shelf terminates at a depth *CLOSEST* to which one of the following?   32._____

    A. 100 feet
    B. 500 feet
    C. 1,000 feet
    D. 2,000 feet

33. Wind gaps are the result of the work of   33._____

    A. glaciers
    B. wind
    C. streams
    D. ocean waves

34. A sea cave at an altitude of 100 feet above sea level indicates a(n)   34._____

    A. great tidal range
    B. land submergence
    C. recent severe storms along the coast
    D. uplift of the land

35. The shortest distance on the earth's surface between New York and London is measured along   35._____

    A. a great circle
    B. an isogonic line
    C. a parallel
    D. a rhumb line

36. Oscillatory waves at sea upon breaking become   36._____

    A. undertow
    B. tsunamis
    C. tidal waves
    D. waves of translation

37. An important east-west fault on Manhattan Island is located along which one of the following?   37._____

    A. 86th Street
    B. 125th Street
    C. 155th Street
    D. Third Avenue

38. The *YOUNGEST* of the following mountain ranges is the   38._____

    A. Adirondacks of New York
    B. Blue Ridge Mountains of Virginia
    C. Green Mountains of Vermont
    D. Sierra Nevada Mountains of California

39. The maximum number of degrees of latitude possible for any place on earth is   39._____

    A. 90
    B. 180
    C. 270
    D. 360

40. The materials of glacial moraines are best described by which one of the following?   40.____

    A. Unassorted, unstratified, rounded
    B. Unassorted, stratified, striated
    C. Unassorted, unstratified, striated
    D. Assorted, stratified, angular

41. Of the following areas the one *NOT* famous for its combination of hot springs and gey-   41.____
sers is

    A. North Island of New Zealand
    B. Iceland
    C. Yellowstone
    D. Yosemite

42. The percentage by weight of the earth's atmosphere that lies below an altitude of 18,000   42.____
feet is *CLOSEST* to which one of the following?

    A. 25%   B. 50%   C. 75%   D. 90%

43. Of the following months, the one in which hurricanes are most likely to strike northeast-   43.____
ern United States is

    A. March   B. May   C. August   D. November

44. The gas produced by the reaction of yeast on glucose is also produced by the reaction   44.____
between

    A. washing soda and limewater
    B. baking soda and water
    C. caustic soda and muriatic acid
    D. baking soda and sour milk

45. Of the following types of clouds, the one *MOST LIKELY* to cause a solar halo is   45.____

    A. cumulonimbus   B. cumulus
    C. cirrostratus   D. stratocumulus

46. The direction of the Northern Hemisphere middle latitude jet stream is principally   46.____

    A. eastward   B. northward   C. southward   D. westward

47. If ten milliliters of hydrogen and ten milliliters of chlorine are placed in a eudiometer and   47.____
exploded, the volume of gas that remains after the reaction is completed is

    A. 2.5 ml.   B. 5 ml.   C. 10 ml.   D. 20 ml.

48. Of the following National Parks, which one is located wholly within the area of an   48.____
exposed batholith?

    A. Yellowstone   B. Grand Canyon
    C. Yosemite   D. Mt. Rainier

49. Residual soil is derived from the weathering of 49.____

    A. flood plain deposits
    B. the underlying bedrock
    C. glacial drift
    D. sand dunes

50. Of the following, the one which is a limestone principally composed of microscopic shells 50.____
and shell fragments cemented together is

    A. chalk   B. travertine
    C. coquina   D. diatomaceous earth

KEY (CORRECT ANSWERS)

1. B	11. C	21. C	31. D	41. D
2. D	12. A	22. C	32. B	42. B
3. B	13. D	23. A	33. C	43. C
4. C	14. B	24. C	34. D	44. D
5. B	15. C	25. A	35. A	45. C
6. D	16. A	26. A	36. D	46. A
7. C	17. C	27. B	37. B	47. D
8. B	18. A	28. D	38. D	48. C
9. D	19. A	29. D	39. A	49. B
10. C	20. A	30. C	40. C	50. A

EXAMINATION SECTION
TEST 1

DIRECTIONS: Each question or incomplete statement is followed by several suggested answers or completions. Select the one that *BEST* answers the question or completes the statement. *PRINT THE LETTER OF THE CORRECT ANSWER IN THE SPACE AT THE RIGHT.*

1. The umbra formed behind the earth by the sun is best explained by which one of the following statements?   1.____

    A. The sun may be considered a point source of light.
    B. Light in space is refracted.
    C. Light rays tend to travel in straight lines.
    D. The earth reflects sunlight.

2. It is generally agreed by scientists that the number of years which have elapsed since the retreat of the last continental ice sheet which covered the northern United States is *CLOSEST* to which one of the following?   2.____

    A. 5000   B. 10,000   C. 15,000   D. 20,000

3. Of the following heavenly bodies, the one on which parachutes would be of *LEAST* value in slowing the landing of a space ship is   3.____

    A. Jupiter   B. Mars   C. Moon   D. Venus

4. Reflection of radio waves for the most part takes place at the atmospheric layer known as the   4.____

    A. ionosphere   B. troposphere
    C. stratosphere   D. aquasphere

5. The distinction between craters and calderas is based on   5.____

    A. their diameters measured from rim to rim
    B. their elevations above the base of volcanoes
    C. their depths below their rims
    D. whether they were formed by explosion or collapse

6. Karst topography is characteristically developed   6.____

    A. in regions covered by sand dunes
    B. in regions underlain by limestones
    C. on terminal moraines
    D. on flood plains

7. Emerald is the gem variety of   7.____

    A. corundum   B. beryl   C. tourmaline   D. quartz

8. Which one of the following rocks reacts by effervescing when a drop of dilute hydrochloric acid is placed on it?   8.____

    A. Siltstone   B. Soapstone
    C. Travertine   D. Gypsum rock

9. Recent age determinations of rocks by radioactive methods have indicated that the time elapsed since the formation of the oldest known rock, expressed in billions of years, is *CLOSEST* to

    A. 1.5   B. 2.5   C. 3.3   D. 4.2

9.____

10. The youthful stage of a rugged shoreline of submergence is characterized by

    A. bay bars   B. offshore bars
    C. barrier beaches   D. lagoons

10.____

11. The average density of the earth was *FIRST* determined experimentally in 1799 by

    A. Priestley   B. Cavendish
    C. Franklin   D. Rutherford

11.____

12. Which one of the following features was formed as a result of glacial action?

    A. Stack   B. Tombolo   C. Drumlin   D. Spit

12.____

13. The chemical composition of the mineral galena is

    A. HgS B. FeS_2 C. PbS D. ZnS

13.____

14. A stream flowing across a coastal plain to the sea would *BEST* be classified as

    A. subsequent   B. antecedent
    C. obsequent   D. consequent

14.____

15. Which one of the following minerals has *PERFECT* cleavage in two directions at right angles to one another?

    A. Hornblende   B. Orthoclase
    C. Calcite   D. Halite

15.____

16. Which one of the following features on the earth's surface was *NOT* formed by the action of erosive agents?

    A. Deflation hollow   B. Graben
    C. Pot hole   D. Sink hole

16.____

17. A glacier is said to be retreating when its glacial ice

    A. reverses its direction of flow
    B. moves downhill at a faster rate than it melts at the terminus
    C. moves downhill at a slower rate than it melts at the terminus
    D. moves downhill at the same rate as it melts at the terminus

17.____

18. The principal ore of tin is

    A. cassiterite   B. chalcopyrite
    C. bauxite   D. sphalerite

18.____

19. Vast quantities of high-grade iron ore have recently been discovered and are now being worked in

    A. the Congo   B. Southern Australia
    C. Central Labrador   D. Central America

19.____

20. The distance of the epicenter of an earthquake from the seismograph recording station can be calculated if one knows the difference in   20._____

    A. time of arrival of the S and L waves
    B. intensity between the P and S waves
    C. time of arrival of the P and S waves
    D. intensity between successive L waves passing the station

21. Of the following processes, which one is important in the formation of metamorphic rocks?   21._____

    A. Solidification   B. Recrystallization
    C. Lithification   D. Evaporation

22. When liquid lava flows into a body of water on the earth's surface, it solidifies into a rock having a characteristic structure called   22._____

    A. ropy   B. pillow   C. cindery   D. vesicular

23. The type of coal commonly found in strongly deformed sedimentary rocks is   23._____

    A. bituminous coal   B. lignite
    C. canned coal   D. anthracite

24. Which one of the following rocks would be *MOST SUITABLE* as an aquifer for an artesian well?   24._____

    A. Granite   B. Shale
    C. Sandstone   D. Limestone

25. Of the following, the group of animals of uncertain biological affinity which became extinct before the end of the Paleozoic Era was the   25._____

    A. trilobites   B. graptolites
    C. blastoids   D. ammonites

26. The brightest star in the nighttime sky of either hemisphere is   26._____

    A. Canopus   B. Capella   C. Sirius   D. Vega

27. Earthshine is seen *BEST* at the phase of the moon called   27._____

    A. first quarter   B. full moon
    C. new crescent   D. old gibbous

28. Of the following physical properties, which one is most useful in distinguishing between pyroxenes and amphiboles?   28._____

    A. Cleavage   B. Luster   C. Color   D. Hardness

29. Tiros I is known as a   29._____

    A. navigation satellite   B. space vehicle
    C. spy-in-the-sky   D. weather satellite

30. Streams flowing straight down the cliff of the Palisades are   30._____

    A. mature   B. subsequent
    C. youthful   D. consequent

31. Which one of the following could be described as a primary sedimentary structure? 31._____

   A. Columnar structure B. Ripple marks
   C. Foliation D. Concretions

32. Of the following minerals, the one which can be scratched by a finger nail is 32._____

   A. calcite B. selenite C. apatite D. fluorite

33. A volcano with a broad base and gentle slopes was formed by the eruption of 33._____

   A. viscous lava
   B. pyroclastic material
   C. fluid lava
   D. alternate fluid lava and pyroclastic material

34. A moraine formed by the confluence of two valley glaciers is a 34._____

   A. terminal moraine B. lateral moraine
   C. medial moraine D. valley train

35. Of the following, the map projection on which all straight lines represent parts of great cir- 35._____
   cles is th

   A. gnomonic B. Mercator
   C. polyconic D. Van der Grinten

36. The mineral raw material used in the manufacture of lead pencils is 36._____

   A. galena B. magnetite
   C. graphite D. native lead

37. The steepest slope of a sand dune faces northwest if the prevailing winds blow from the 37._____

   A. northwest B. northeast
   C. southwest D. southeast

38. No alpine glaciers exist in 38._____

   A. Africa B. South America
   C. Australia D. Europe

39. A study of captured specimens of a group of fishes called the coelacanths, once consid- 39._____
   ered extinct, confirmed the belief that they possessed

   A. an armor-plated head
   B. rudimentary legs instead of fins
   C. a primitive air-breathing apparatus
   D. no jaws

40. Of the following plateaus, the one which was formed PRINCIPALLY by lava flows is the 40._____
   plateau known as

   A. Allegheny B. Columbia
   C. Colorado D. Piedmont

41. Which one of the following major orogenies in the geologic history of North America   41.____
occurred more than 600 million years ago according to scientists?

    A. Appalachian   B. Laramide
    C. Laurentian   D. Cascadian

42. Naturally cemented gravel forms a rock called   42.____

    A. breccia   B. tuff
    C. conglomerate   D. sandstone

43. The deepest known spot on earth is located   43.____

    A. off the coast of Lower California
    B. off the eastern coast of Japan
    C. in the Marianas trench east of the Philippines
    D. in the Puerto Rico trench in the Caribbean Sea

44. Graptolites, believed to have been planktonic animals probably   44.____

    A. floated in the open ocean
    B. lived attached to the ocean bottom
    C. lived as crawlers on the ocean bottom
    D. were active swimmers in the open ocean

45. Which one of the following was the result of a concordant, igneous intrusion?   45.____

    A. Dike   B. Batholith   C. Laccolith   D. Xenolith

46. The branches into which a river divides as it flows over a delta are known as   46.____

    A. tributaries   B. dendrites
    C. distributaries   D. estuaries

47. The recent discovery of abundant fossils in rocks of Pre-cambrian age in South Australia   47.____
is significant chiefly because it

    A. supplies evidence which is contrary to the generally accepted doctrines of evolution
    B. represents a rare example of the preservation of fossils in highly metamorphosed rocks
    C. is the first time that bona fide fossils of Pre-cambrian age have been found
    D. furnishes proof that the Precambrian oceans contained a great variety of soft-bodied animals some of which do not resemble any other known organism

48. The topography of the bottom of the Atlantic Ocean basin is characterized by the presence of   48.____

    A. vast stretches of featureless plains
    B. rugged relief features some of which rise more than 10,000 feet above the ocean floor
    C. a great number of flat-topped seamounts separated by little-dissected plains
    D. an undulating surface of low relief traversed by occasional deep trenches

49. Of the following, the one which some scientists have considered a result of the contraction of the earth's crust is   49._____

    A. elevation of plateau regions thousands of feet above sea level
    B. formation of folded mountain ranges
    C. origin of fjords and estuaries
    D. formation of vast epicontinental seas in the interior of North America during Paleozoic time

50. A rock formed by contact metamorphism of shale is   50._____

    A. hornfels   B. slate   C. marble   D. gneiss

————

KEY (CORRECT ANSWERS)

1.	C	11.	B	21.	B	31.	B	41.	C
2.	B	12.	C	22.	B	32.	B	42.	C
3.	C	13.	C	23.	D	33.	C	43.	C
4.	A	14.	D	24.	C	34.	C	44.	A
5.	A	15.	B	25.	B	35.	A	45.	C
6.	B	16.	B	26.	C	36.	C	46.	C
7.	B	17.	C	27.	C	37.	D	47.	D
8.	C	18.	A	28.	A	38.	C	48.	B
9.	C	19.	C	29.	D	39.	C	49.	B
10.	A	20.	C	30.	C	40.	B	50.	A

————

TEST 2

DIRECTIONS: Each question or incomplete statement is followed by several suggested answers or completions. Select the one that *BEST* answers the question or completes the statement. *PRINT THE LETTER OF THE CORRECT ANSWER IN THE SPACE AT THE RIGHT.*

1. Folding of sediments usually involves   1.____

   A. uplift by igneous intrusions
   B. differential stretching of individual beds
   C. crustal lengthening
   D. sliding of individual beds past each other

2. The location of latitude 42° N and longitude 74° W is in the state of   2.____

   A. Nevada   B. Michigan   C. New York   D. Florida

3. The geographical center of the Antartic continent is known as the   3.____

   A. true south pole
   B. geomagnetic south pole
   C. pole of inaccessibility
   D. geophysical south pole

4. The geological period noteworthy for the formation of extensive salt deposits is the   4.____

   A. Cambrian   B. Eocene
   C. Mississippian   D. Silurian

5. The two geologic periods which were *NOT* consecutive are   5.____

   A. Cambrian and Ordovician
   B. Silurian and Devonian
   C. Devonian and Permian
   D. Mississippian and Pennsylvanian

6. The first abundant fossil record is found in rocks of the   6.____

   A. Cretaceous Period   B. Cambrian Period
   C. Triassic Period   D. Ordovician Period

7. The "Law of Original Horizontality" of sedimentary rocks was *FIRST* stated by 7.____

   A. Galileo   B. Agassiz   C. deSaussure   D. Steno

8. An animal thought to have been extinct for some 60 million years has been discovered   8.____
   still living off the coast of Madagascar. It belongs to a group known as

   A. trilobites   B. coelacanths
   C. graptolites   D. plesiosaurs

9. The most recent estimate of the time in years elapsed since the retreat of the last ice   9.____
   sheet from the vicinity of New York City is, approximately,

   A. 2500   B. 5000   C. 10,000   D. 15,000

10. The most reliable method of determining geologic time is based on the   10.____

    A. salt content in the sea
    B. accumulated thickness of sediments
    C. disintegration of radioactive minerals
    D. rate of erosion of the land

11. The deep sea floor of the Atlantic Ocean between North America and Europe   11.____

    A. has a highly varied topography including at least one major north-south trending mountain range
    B. is a nearly featureless plain
    C. has several trenches reaching depths of over 6 miles
    D. is characterized by numerous flat-topped submarine mountain peaks, called guyots, which rise from level plateaus

12. The most effective method of preventing spring floods in large stream systems like the Mississippi River Basin is   12.____

    A. construction of a large dam across the main stream
    B. building larger and higher artificial levees
    C. deepening the channel of the main stream by dredging
    D. construction of many smaller dams across tributary stream valleys

13. Arkose differs from ordinary sandstones in being richer in   13.____

    A. calcite   B. feldspar   C. mica   D. fossils

14. Taconite is a relatively new but important source of   14.____

    A. cobalt   B. iron   C. molybdenum   D. tungsten

15. A rock which contains phenocrysts is said to be   15.____

    A. aphanitic   B. phaneritic
    C. porphyritic   D. vitric

16. A mineral with rhombohedral cleavage is   16.____

    A. calcite   B. feldspar   C. garnet   D. talc

17. Present isostatic conditions are checked from time to time by precise measurements of   17.____

    A. the acceleration due to gravity
    B. the mass of mountain ranges
    C. plumb bob deflections
    D. sea level changes

18. $2KAlSi_3O_8 + H_2CO_3 + nH_2O = K_2CO_3 + Al_2(OH)_2Si_4O_{10} \cdot nH_2O + 2SiO_2$ 18.____
This equation expresses the changes which occur upon chemical weathering of

    A. plagioclase feldspar   B. olivine
    C. orthoclase feldspar   D. biotite

19. In the United States, alpine glaciers occur on   19.____

    A. Harney Peak, Black Hills
    B. Mt. Washington, White Mts.
    C. Mt. Rainier, Washington
    D. Mt. Marcy, Adirondack Mts.

20. A black mineral whose streak is red is   20.____

    A. augite   B. hematite
    C. magnetite   D. uraninite

21. All of the following minerals are micas *EXCEPT*   21.____

    A. biotite   B. celestite
    C. muscovite   D. phlogopite

22. Diorite consists largely of the minerals   22.____

    A. quartz and orthoclase
    B. orthoclase and hornblende
    C. plagioclase and hornblende
    D. augite and plagioclase

23. An igneous rock in which light-colored minerals predominate is   23.____

    A. andesite   B. peridotite
    C. phyllite   D. rhyolite

24. The maximum depth in feet of glacial ice recorded in the Antarctic was about   24.____

    A. 9,000   B. 14,000   C. 17,000   D. 21,000

25. A form of bedrock found in Staten Island but not in the other boroughs of New York City is   25.____

    A. conglomerate   B. rhyolite
    C. serpentine   D. syenite

26. The "blackerths" of the American prairies are classified by soil scientists as   26.____

    A. laterites   B. pedalfers
    C. pedocals   D. sials

27. From the Fall Line westward at Richmond, Virginia, the sequence of physiographic   27.
regions is

    A. Piedmont, Valley and Ridge Province, Appalachian Plateau, Blue Ridge
    B. Piedmont, Blue Ridge, Valley and Ridge Province, Appalachian Plateau
    C. Piedmont, Valley and Ridge Province, Blue Ridge, Appalachian Plateau
    D. Piedmont, Blue Ridge, Appalachian Plateau, Valley and Ridge Province

28. A city located on the Fall Line of eastern United States is   28.____

    A. Atlanta, Ga.   B. Atlantic City, N. J.
    C. Boston, Mass.   D. Philadelphia, Pa.

29. The Watchung Ridges of New Jersey originated through 　　29.____

    A. faulting   B. folding
    C. glacial action   D. vulcanism

30. The Great Valley of the Valley and Ridge Province of eastern United States is underlain 　　30.____
by

    A. conglomerate   B. limestone
    C. sandstone   D. shale

31. In general, the alluvial deposit with the steepest slope is the 　　31.____

    A. alluvial fan   B. delta
    C. flood plain   D. till plain

32. Structurally, a hogback is most closely related to a 　　32.____

    A. butte   B. cuesta   C. mesa   D. neck

33. The bergschrund is a 　　33.____

    A. crevasse at the head of a glacier
    B. lake at the base of a mountain
    C. fissure in a cliff
    D. boulder field

34. A rock whose presence in Manhattan is best explained as the result of glacial action is 　　34.____

    A. diabase   B. dolomite   C. gneiss   D. schist

35. A glacial deposit which consists of unstratified materials is the 　　35.____

    A. drumlin   B. esker
    C. kame   D. valley train

36. Annular drainage patterns are found in the 　　36.____

    A. Atlantic Coastal Plain
    B. Ridge and Valley Province
    C. Piedmont Upland
    D. Black Hills of South Dakota

37. The drainage pattern typical of a region of folded structure is 　　37.____

    A. annular   B. dendritic   C. radial   D. trellis

38. At Delaware Water Gap, Pennsylvania, the Delaware River is said to be 　　38.____

    A. antecedent   B. obsequent
    C. subsequent   D. superimposed

39. The San Juan River in Utah is most noted for its 　　39.____

    A. braided pattern   B. stream piracy features
    C. alluvial cones   D. entrenched meanders

40. To a depth of some 100 miles below the earth's surface, the velocities of earthquake waves

    A. increase steadily
    B. increase at variable rates
    C. decrease steadily
    D. are essentially constant

40.____

41. For the most part, the valleys of Manhattan and the Bronx are developed in the bedrock known as

    A. Fordham gneiss   B. Inwood marble
    C. Manhattan schist   D. Yonkers granite

41.____

42. A "mountain" region with horizontal rock structure is the

    A. Catskills of New York State
    B. Adirondacks of New York State
    C. Ramapos of New York State
    D. Hudson Highlands

42.____

43. The erogenic disturbance which occurred at the close of the Paleozoic Era is that which produced the

    A. Appalachian Mountains
    B. Rocky Mountains
    C. Sierra Nevada Mountains
    D. Taconics

43.____

44. An example of a waterfall caused by a lava dike is

    A. the Great Falls of the Potomac
    B. Niagara Falls
    C. Lower Yellowstone Falls
    D. Yosemite Falls

44.____

45. Barchanes are

    A. crescentic sand dunes   B. desert sandstorms
    C. mushroom rocks   D. wind-eroded depressions

45.____

46. Dreikanter are

    A. pebbles shaped by wind abrasion
    B. mountain peaks shaped by glacial erosion
    C. sand dunes formed by variable winds
    D. angles of mineral crystals

46.____

47. In an anticlinal formation of oil, salt water, and gas, the arrangement of materials from the top downward is

    A. oil, gas, salt water   B. oil, salt water, gas
    C. gas, oil, salt water   D. gas, salt water, oil

47.____

48. Half Dome in Yosemite National Park is a noted example of a(n) 48.____

    A. domed mountain   B. exfoliation dome
    C. truncated volcano   D. matterhorn peak

49. The term "graben" is synonymous with a(n) 49.____

    A. block mountain   B. fault-block valley
    C. fault line   D. elevated fault block

50. Our present knowledge of the interior of the earth was largely acquired from studies of 50.____

    A. earthquake waves   B. deep mines and oil wells
    C. elements in the sun   D. volcanic eruptions

KEY (CORRECT ANSWERS)

1. D	11. A	21. B	31. A	41. B
2. C	12. D	22. C	32. B	42. A
3. C	13. B	23. D	33. A	43. A
4. D	14. B	24. B	34. A	44. C
5. C	15. C	25. C	35. A	45. A
6. B	16. A	26. C	36. D	46. A
7. D	17. A	27. B	37. D	47. C
8. B	18. C	28. D	38. D	48. B
9. C	19. C	29. D	39. D	49. B
10. C	20. B	30. B	40. B	50. A

TEST 3

DIRECTIONS: Each question or incomplete statement is followed by several suggested answers or completions. Select the one that *BEST* answers the question or completes the statement. *PRINT THE LETTER OF THE CORRECT ANSWER IN THE SPACE AT THE RIGHT.*

1. Dikes are distinguished from sills by the fact that they　　　　　　　1._____

    A. cut across the structure of the country rocks
    B. are vertical or near-vertical in attitude
    C. fill fractures in the country rocks
    D. are intrusive in origin

2. Lava flows which issued from long fissures in the ground were responsible for the formation of the　　　　　　2._____

    A. Palisades   B. Colorado Plateau
    C. Columbia Plateau   D. Allegheny Plateau

3. A volcano which erupted with extreme violence in the 20th century is　　　　3._____

    A. Mauna Loa   B. Mt. Pelee
    C. Vesuvius   D. Mt. Lassen

4. Batholiths　　　　　　　　　　　　　　　　　　　　　4._____

    A. are generally composed of basalts
    B. have known floors
    C. are extrusions associated with periods and regions of great stability of the earth's crust
    D. are intrusions associated with periods and regions of great instability of the earth's crust

5. Pillow structures in lava flows indicate that the lava was　　　　　　5._____

    A. extruded into water or over wet ground
    B. deeply weathered after solidification
    C. affected by earth movements after solidification
    D. erupted explosively from a volcano

6. A mountain range which is still in the process of being folded is the　　　　6._____

    A. Sierra Nevada
    B. Alps
    C. Coast Range of California
    D. Ural Mountains

7. Petrology is a branch of Geology which is concerned with the study of　　　　7._____

    A. oil and gas   B. landforms
    C. fossils   D. rocks

8. The chemical composition of the mineral gypsum is　　　　　　　8._____

    A. $CaCO_3$ B. $CaSO_4 \cdot 2H_2O$ C. $CaSiO_4$ D. CaF_2

9. The space lattice structure of minerals was discovered by the study of crystals using the   9.____
   method of

    A. chemical analysis   B. spectrographic methods
    C. x-ray diffraction   D. electron microscopy

10. An igneous rock composed of 60% feldspar, 25% quartz and 15% hornblende and hav-   10.____
    ing a phaneritic texture, is

    A. diorite   B. basalt   C. granite   D. gabbro

11. Kettle holes are the result of   11.____

    A. melting of ice blocks buried in terminal moraines
    B. solution of limestones by ground water
    C. wind action on loose desert sands
    D. abrasion by whirl pools in stream channels

12. A rock structure which is the result of metamorphism is   12.____

    A. columnar structure   B. vesicular structure
    C. stratification   D. foliation

13. Entrenched meanders indicate that a stream   13.____

    A. is in its first cycle of erosion
    B. has been rejuvenated
    C. is flowing on a peneplane
    D. is flowing on limestone

14. Wind-abraded pebbles are characteristically   14.____

    A. well rounded   B. striated
    C. faceted   D. spherical

15. Permeability of a sandstone layer is a measure of its   15.____

    A. total pore space
    B. grain size
    C. ability to hold water
    D. ability to discharge water

16. The earliest known glacial interval occurred during the   16.____

    A. Cambrian Period   B. Pre-Cambrian Era
    C. Pleistocene Epoch   D. Permian Period

17. A rock which indicates a desert climate at the time of its formation is   17.____

    A. loess   B. tillite   C. limestone   D. shale

18. Streams in their youthful stage of development can be recognized by the presence of   18.____

    A. meanders   B. rapids
    C. oxbow lakes   D. flood plains

19. A mineral having the following properties--yellow color, metallic luster, greenish-black streak and hardness 6--is   19.____

    A. gold   B. sulfur   C. pyrite   D. limonite

20. The most effective weathering process in the New York City area is   20.____

    A. oxidation   B. exfoliation
    C. wedge-work of ice   D. wedge-work of plants

21. A rock formed by contact metamorphism is   21.____

    A. slate   B. schist   C. gneiss   D. hornfels

22. The important feature of distinction between a conglomerate and a sandstone is   22.____

    A. composition   B. texture
    C. fossil content   D. color

23. Mountain glaciers   23.____

    A. are capable of carving their own valleys
    B. follow pre-existing stream valleys
    C. have a tendency to subdue the pre-existing topography
    D. leave their deposits in the form of drumlins

24. Glaciers are said to be retreating when   24.____

    A. the rate of melting at the terminus exceeds the rate of ice flow
    B. the rate of ice flow exceeds the rate of melting at the terminus
    C. the direction of ice flow is reversed
    D. the ice flow becomes incapable of overriding the terminal moraine

25. Shore lines which were initially formed by submergence may be found in   25.____

    A. Florida   B. Maine   C. Hawaii   D. Bermuda

26. It is *INCORRECT* to state that large lakes   26.____

    A. act as settling basins for sediments
    B. have a modifying influence upon the climate of the surrounding region
    C. are permanent features of the landscape
    D. may turn saline when their outlets are blocked

27. Savannah, Georgia, lies in the Physiographic Province known as the   27.____

    A. Triassic Lowland   B. Piedmont
    C. Atlantic Coastal Plain   D. Gulf Coastal Plain

28. The essential difference between plains and plateaus is   28.____

    A. the erosive agent responsible for their formation
    B. their areal extent
    C. the structure of the rocks underlying them
    D. their elevation above sea level

29. The Sierra Nevada is a mountain region formed principally by   29.____

    A. folding
    B. volcanic eruptions
    C. block-faulting
    D. erosion of horizontal strata

30. Longshore currents are the result of   30.____

    A. waves striking the shore perpendicular to the coast line
    B. waves striking the shore oblique to the coast line
    C. winds blowing from land to sea
    D. temperature convection currents in the near-shore portions of the ocean

31. A glacial deposit whose form and shape does *NOT* reveal the general direction of glacial   31.____
    motion is a(n)

    A. ground moraine   B. terminal moraine
    C. esker   D. drumlin

32. The contact between the Triassic sandstones and shales of New Jersey and the crystal-   32.____
    line metamorphic rocks of New York City beneath the Hudson River is

    A. conformable   B. gradational
    C. uncohformable   D. a fault contact

33. A mineral characterized by a single direction of perfect cleavage is   33.____

    A. albite   B. magnetite   C. muscovite   D. augite

34. A common accessory mineral in the mica schist of New York City is   34.____

    A. diopside   B. garnet   C. magnetite   D. olivine

35. The youngest rock found in the bedrock underlying Manhattan Island is   35.____

    A. mica schist   B. hornblende schist
    C. biotite gneiss   D. granite pegmatite

36. Sapphire is the gem variety of the mineral   36.____

    A. beryl   B. topaz   C. microcline   D. corundum

37. Plaster of Paris is made by heating the mineral   37.____

    A. gypsum   B. orthoclase   C. halite   D. calcite

38. The principal ingredient of scouring powder is   38.____

    A. quartz   B. feldspar   C. kaolin   D. calcite

39. Abandoned magnetite mines in the Adirondack Mts. of New York have been reopened in   39.____
    recent years for the recovery of

    A. titanium   B. iron   C. copper   D. lead

40. Large reserves of low-grade uranium deposits have been found in   40.____

    A. Northern Canada   B. Venezuela
    C. Labrador   D. Colorado

41. Galena is an ore of   41._____

    A. copper   B. iron   C. lead   D. zinc

42. The Alaska Current in the Northern Pacific Ocean   42._____

    A. drifts in a westerly direction
    B. is a cold water current
    C. tempers the climate of the southern coast of Alaska
    D. is a northward extension of the Peru current

43. In the oceanic circulation along the coast of South America,   43._____

    A. both the Peru and Brazil currents flow northward
    B. both the Peru and Brazil currents flow southward
    C. the Peru Current flows northward, but the Brazil Current flows southward
    D. the Peru Current flows southward, but the Brazil Current flows northward

44. The Greenland Current flows   44._____

    A. southward along Greenland's eastern coast
    B. northward along Greenland's eastern coast
    C. southward along Greenland's western coast
    D. northward along Greenland's western coast

45. Among the following statements about corals, the only *CORRECT* one is: 45._____

    A. Corals grow in either fresh or salt water.
    B. Corals require a water temperature of not less than 78° F.
    C. Corals grow best on the side of a reef exposed to waves and currents.
    D. Corals will not grow at depths exceeding 50 feet.

46. An example of a neutral shoreline, according to a genetic classification, is the   46._____

    A. delta shoreline   B. ria shoreline
    C. fiord shoreline   D. coastal plain shoreline

47. An example of a spit is   47._____

    A. Atlantic City   B. Jones Beach
    C. Fire Island   D. Rockaway Beach

48. The countercurrent discovered beneath the Gulf Stream is   48._____

    A. 9,000 feet down, and moves 8 miles a day
    B. 9,000 feet down, and moves 8 miles an hour
    C. 1,900 feet down, and moves 8 miles an hour
    D. 1,900 feet down, and moves 8 miles a day

49. Explorations have disclosed the existence of a vast area of bottom sludge rich in manga-   49._____
nese, iron, copper, and cobalt in the

    A. Antarctic Ocean   B. South Atlantic Ocean
    C. Indian Ocean   D. Southwest Pacific Ocean

50. The diameter of the earth at the equator is greater than that measured from North to   50.____
South pole because of the earth's

    A. revolution around the sun
    B. rotation on its axis
    C. magnetic field
    D. gravitative attraction by the moon

————

KEY (CORRECT ANSWERS)

1. A	11. A	21. D	31. A	41. C
2. C	12. D	22. B	32. C	42. C
3. B	13. B	23. B	33. C	43. C
4. D	14. C	24. A	34. B	44. A
5. A	15. D	25. B	35. D	45. C
6. C	16. B	26. C	36. D	46. A
7. D	17. A	27. C	37. A	47. D
8. B	18. B	28. D	38. B	48. A
9. C	19. C	29. C	39. A	49. D
10. C	20. C	30. B	40. D	50. B

————

TEST 4

DIRECTIONS: Each question or incomplete statement is followed by several suggested answers or completions. Select the one that *BEST* answers the question or completes the statement. *PRINT THE LETTER OF THE CORRECT ANSWER IN THE SPACE AT THE RIGHT.*

1. Deposition of sediments by streams requires that   1.____

   A. stream load exceed stream capacity
   B. stream load equal stream capacity
   C. stream load be less than stream capacity
   D. the regional base level be dropping

2. The small stream flowing down the face of the Palisades cliff may be classified as   2.____

   A. obsequent   B. subsequent
   C. consequent   D. resequent

3. Great Salt Lake in Utah   3.____

   A. lies below sea level
   B. is the remnant of a former fresh water lake
   C. is fed by ocean water
   D. lies in a region where rainfall exceeds evaporation

4. Canada produces more than 85% of the world's supply of   4.____

   A. radium   B. tungsten   C. nickel   D. iron

5. An important industry in the Adirondact Mts. of New York State is the mining of ores of 5.____

   A. copper   B. gold   C. nickel   D. titanium

6. Manhattan Island lies in the Physiographic Province known as the   6.____

   A. Atlantic Coastal Plain   B. Triassic Lowland
   C. Appalachian Plateau   D. New England Upland

7. The term "Karst topography" is used to describe a region of   7.____

   A. glacial troughs and cirques
   B. limestone bedrock and underground drainage
   C. sand dunes and desert pavement
   D. volcanoes and lava flows

8. An ocean current that flows southward is the   8.____

   A. Benguela Current   B. Canary Current
   C. Gulf Stream   D. Japan Current

9. A psychrometer consists of one   9.____

   A. mercurial and one alcohol thermometer
   B. aneroid and one mercurial barometer
   C. dry bulb and one wet bulb thermometer
   D. maximum and one minimum thermometer

10. A Mediterranean climate is characterized by   10._____

    A. rainy winters and dry summers
    B. dry winters and dry summers
    C. dry winters and rainy summers
    D. rainy winters and rainy summers

11. The cause of the phases of the moon is the   11._____

    A. revolution of the earth
    B. revolution of the moon
    C. rotation of the earth
    D. rotation of the moon

12. The earth in its orbit reaches aphelion about   12._____

    A. January 1   B. April 1   C. July 1   D. October 1

13. Halos around the moon and the sun are usually caused by the type of cloud called   13._____

    A. cumulus   B. cirro-cumulus
    C. cirro-stratus   D. strato-cumulus

14. The apparent visual magnitude of the North Star (Polaris) is   14._____

    A. -1   B. 1   C. 2   D. 3

15. A mountain peak well known as both a monadnock and an exfoliation dome is   15._____

    A. Pike's Peak Colorado
    B. Mt. Rushmore, South Dakota
    C. Mt. Washington, New Hampshire
    D. Stone Mt., Georgia

16. When the limbs of a rock fold are parallel, the fold is described as   16._____

    A. monoclinal   B. recumbent
    C. isoclinal   D. unwarped

17. The angle between the dip and strike of an outcrop is *ALWAYS*   17._____

    A. acute   B. obtuse   C. right   D. straight

18. The Palisades of New Jersey are a feature of the physiographic region known as the   18._____

    A. New England Province
    B. Older Appalachians
    C. Triassic Lowland
    D. Valley and Ridge Province

19. A region of strongly dissected horizontal or nearly horizontal strata is the   19._____

    A. Adirondack Mountains   B. Catskill Mountains
    C. Piedmont Upland   D. Ramapo Mountains

20. The rate at which the temperature of the earth's crust increases with depth is approximately 1° F for every   20._____

    A. 50 feet to 75 feet   B. 200 feet to 300 feet
    C. 900 feet to 1000 feet   D. 1/2 mile

21. A stack is an erosion remnant resulting from the action of   21._____

    A. glaciers   B. streams   C. waves   D. winds

22. A bergschrund is a(n)   22._____

    A. cavern   B. cirque
    C. glacial crevasse   D. alpine lake

23. A crescent-shaped sand dune is called a   23._____

    A. barchane   B. bolson   C. horst   D. pediment

24. Slickensides result from   24._____

    A. faulting   B. glacial action
    C. igneous activity   D. weathering

25. Alluvial fans tend to form   25._____

    A. at the base of a prominent cliff by mass wasting
    B. where streams enter quiet bodies of water
    C. where continental glaciers have piled up prominent terminal moraines
    D. where streams emerge from mountain canyons

26. In the struggle of processes tending to shape the present earth's surface,   26._____

    A. antigradation is more effective than gradation
    B. the effects of gradation and antigradation are approximately balanced
    C. gradation is more effective than antigradation
    D. gradation and antigradation are negligible factors

27. The plunge of a fold measures the inclination of   27._____

    A. its axial plane
    B. either limb
    C. its axis of folding
    D. the overturned limb only

28. Of the following sedimentary structures the one most useful in determining whether a stratum in the field is right side up or overturned is   28._____

    A. current ripple marks   B. concretions
    C. oolites   D. mud cracks

29. The Sierra Nevada of California is an example of a mountain range   29._____

    A. composed of a series of volcanoes
    B. carved out of thick lava flows by the action of water and glacial ice
    C. formed by block faulting
    D. formed by intense folding and thrust faulting

30. The *FIRST* step in the mountain building sequence of folded mountains is   30._____

    A. folding
    B. isostatic adjustment
    C. formation of a geosyncline
    D. igneous activity

31. A landform developed by sub-aerial erosion in a region of horizontal strata is a   31._____

    A. hogback   B. butte
    C. roche moutonnee   D. drumlin

32. The inferred layered structure of the earth's interior is largely based on   32._____

    A. distinct changes in travel time of earthquake waves at certain depths
    B. calculations of the average density of the earth
    C. gravimetric measurements from submarines
    D. measurements of the earth's magnetic field

33. The geologic age of a peneplane is *BEST* determined by   33._____

    A. finding the ages of the oldest rocks bevelled by the peneplane and the youngest rocks covering it
    B. finding the ages of the youngest rocks bevelled by it and the oldest rocks covering it
    C. the present stage of dissection of the peneplane
    D. the maturity of the soil covering the peneplane

34. A peneplane of considerable slope results from   34._____

    A. a diastrophic change
    B. glaciation
    C. a change in sea level
    D. the normal cycle of erosion

35. The youthful stage of a rugged shoreline of submergence is characterized by   35._____

    A. tombolos   B. offshore bars
    C. lagoons   D. barrier beaches

36. A ria shoreline is formed by the   36._____

    A. emergence of a lake floor
    B. partial submergence of a stream-dissected land mass
    C. formation of an alluvial fan in a gulf
    D. stream erosion of a newly formed continental shelf

37. The most steeply inclined beds of a delta are known as   37._____

    A. fore-set   B. bottom-set
    C. hind-set   D. top-set

38. Entrenched meanders are formed when   38._____

    A. an old river is rejuvenated
    B. a young river matures

C. subsidence occurs in a young river valley
D. subsidence occurs in an old river valley

39. A river that maintained its course through a rising mountain range is said to be   39.____

   A. antecedent   B. ancestral
   C. inherited   D. superimposed

40. When subsequent tributaries develop at right angles to a consequent master stream, the   40.____
    resulting drainage pattern is described as

   A. dendritic   B. insequent
   C. radial   D. trellis

41. In late Triassic time, the eastern United States was subjected to   41.____

   A. marine sedimentation
   B. continental sedimentation
   C. peneplanation
   D. orogenic mountain building

42. A cycle of stream erosion is   42.____

   A. the swinging of a stream channel from side to side in a broad valley
   B. the movement of water from the sea to the land through the atmosphere
   C. a seasonal variation of flood and low water stages
   D. a sequence of marked valley changes over a long period of time

43. In graded bedding, examined from bottom to top, one may expect to find sediments rang-   43.____
    ing from

   A. gravel to sand to mud
   B. fine sand to coarse sand to mud
   C. mud to sand to gravel
   D. sand to gravel to mud

44. Development of cross-bedding is LEAST likely to occur in sedimentary deposits laid   44.____
    down by

   A. wind   B. streams
   C. ocean currents   D. glacial ice

45. Dendritic drainage is developed on   45.____

   A. folded strata   B. a structural dome
   C. horizontal strata   D. a volcanic cone

46. A stream becomes permanent only   46.____

   A. after its bed has been cut below the water table
   B. after it has become graded
   C. when it reaches base level
   D. when it attains old age

47. According to most recent explorations, the maximum thickness, in feet, of glacial ice in Antarctica is approximately

      A. 5,000   B. 10,000   C. 15,000   D. 20,000

47.____

48. We should not expect to find, on the Palisades ridge, glacial erratics consisting of

      A. crystalline rocks of the Hudson Highlands
      B. Manhattan schist
      C. Palisades diabase
      D. red sandstones of the Newark Series

48.____

49. The National Park, famous for its features developed by valley glaciations, is

      A. Yosemite   B. Yellowstone
      C. Grand Canyon   D. Carlsbad

49.____

50. An erosional feature resulting from continental glaciation is a(n)

      A. terminal moraine   B. esker
      C. cirque   D. roche moutonnée

50.____

KEY (CORRECT ANSWERS)

1.	A	11.	B	21.	C	31.	B	41.	B
2.	A	12.	C	22.	C	32.	A	42.	D
3.	B	13.	C	23.	A	33.	B	43.	A
4.	C	14.	C	24.	A	34.	A	44.	C
5.	D	15.	D	25.	D	35.	A	45.	C
6.	D	16.	C	26.	A	36.	B	46.	A
7.	B	17.	C	27.	C	37.	A	47.	B
8.	B	18.	C	28.	D	38.	A	48.	B
9.	C	19.	B	29.	C	39.	A	49.	A
10.	A	20.	A	30.	C	40.	D	50.	D

EXAMINATION SECTION
TEST 1

DIRECTIONS: Each question or incomplete statement is followed by several suggested answers or completions. Select the one that BEST answers the question or completes the statement. *PRINT THE LETTER OF THE CORRECT ANSWER IN THE SPACE AT THE RIGHT.*

1. The Kansan, Nebraskan, Illinoisan, and Wisconsin epochs were noted for which one of the following?

    A. Widespread volcanic activity
    B. Spread of vast ice sheets
    C. Unusual deposition in geosynclines
    D. Mountain building on a huge scale

  1____

2. Barchons are defined as

    A. tracks produced by prehistoric animals
    B. large deposits of glacial till
    C. sand dunes shaped like a crescent
    D. fragments of igneous rock

  2____

3. The presence of trilobite fossils dates rocks as belonging to which one of the following eras?

    A. Precambrian   B. Paleozoic
    C. Mesozoic   D. Cenozoic

  3____

4. The color of the streak that results when pyrite is rubbed across a porcelain plate is

    A. yellow   B. brown   C. green   D. black

  4____

5. Which one of the following would be POOREST for showing cleavage?

    A. Mica   B. Calcite   C. Feldspar   D. Obsidian

  5____

6. Natural cement is composed MAINLY of which one of the following?

    A. Sandstone   B. Silica
    C. Calcium carbonate   D. Loess

  6____

7. Of the following, the rock whose mineral content MOST strongly resembles that of granite is

    A. obsidian   B. rhyolite   C. andesite   D. limestone

  7____

8. Of the following, which series presents transporting agents in the order of their carrying power?

    A. Running water - oscillating water - wind - ice
    B. Ice - running water - oscillating water - wind
    C. Oscillating water - running water - wind - ice
    D. Wind - ice - running water - oscillating water

  8____

9. Rock masses which were produced when the magma solidified below the surface are called which one of the following?

    A. Plutons
    B. Basalts
    C. Lateral moraines
    D. Erratics

9____

10. Stalactites and stalagmites are forms of which one of the following?

    A. Travertine
    B. Calcium bicarbonate
    C. Gypsum
    D. Silica

10____

11. Fossils are rarely found in the bedrock of New York City because

    A. the rocks pre-date the period of skeletal life forms
    B. repeated glacial invasion has removed all traces
    C. metamorphism has destroyed any evidence of life
    D. the rocks are all igneous

11____

12. Which one of the following is the cause of the red coloring in many sedimentary rocks?

    A. Calcite   B. Hematite   C. Pyrite   D. Silica

12____

13. Recent studies of the sea floor indicate the widespread prevalence of cannon-ball shaped nodules of

    A. zinc   B. antimony   C. manganese   D. zirconium

13____

14. Of the following, a factor that does NOT directly affect the direction of ocean currents is

    A. prevailing winds
    B. rotation of the earth
    C. temperature of the water
    D. outline of continents

14____

15. A flat-topped submarine mountain whose summit has been planed away to the surface of the ocean is called a(n)

    A. offlap   B. guyot   C. nummulite   D. reef

15____

16. Of the following, the one that is NOT an ore of copper is

    A. chalcopyrite
    B. malachite
    C. azurite
    D. sphalerite

16____

17. Which one of the following is a speleologist?

    A. Mountain climber
    B. Deep sea diver
    C. Archeologist
    D. Cave explorer

17____

18. In which one of the following places is the movement of a valley glacier GREATEST? Its

    A. bottom
    B. valley walls
    C. top and center
    D. large crevasses

18____

19. To which one of the following does the process of cavitation in geology refer?

    A. Filling of cavities by groundwater
    B. Slope erosion
    C. Pothole migration
    D. Collapse of vapor bubbles in water

19____

20. Geosynclinal deposits that reach a thickness of 50,000 ft. have, in most cases, been deposited in marine waters having a depth CLOSEST to which one of the following? _____ feet.

    A. 1,000   B. 10,000   C. 30,000   D. 50,000

20_____

21. The northernmost boundary of the zone of Middle Latitude Climate is marked by the

    A. January Average Isotherm of 50°F
    B. July Average Isotherm of 50°F
    C. Annual Average Isotherm of 50°F
    D. Annual Average Isotherm of 60°F

21_____

22. In desert regions, pebbles found there which are scoured into flat-sided, sharp-edged forms are called

    A. dreikanters   B. playas   C. aretes   D. barchanes

22_____

23. The complexity of formulas of the silicates is BEST explained in terms of

    A. excess of negative ions in a tetrahedron crystal lattice
    B. excess of positive ions in a tetrahedron crystal lattice
    C. the unfilled spaces in its rhombohedron structure
    D. a fluctuating valence among its ions

23_____

24. The dip of a rock structure refers to which one of the following?

    A. The angle of junction of two deformed and adjacent rock layers
    B. The direction of the line of intersection of the layer with the horizontal plane
    C. The angle that the rock layer makes with a north-south line
    D. Inclination of the stratum from the horizontal plane

24_____

25. In the chemical weathering of orthoclase, which one of the following takes place?

    A. Only clay is produced.
    B. Clay and finely divided quartz are produced.
    C. Clay and calcite are produced.
    D. Calcite and quartz are produced.

25_____

———————

KEY (CORRECT ANSWERS)

1.	B		11.	C
2.	C		12.	B
3.	B		13.	C
4.	D		14.	C
5.	D		15.	B
6.	C		16.	D
7.	B		17.	D
8.	B		18.	C
9.	A		19.	D
10.	A		20.	A

21.	B
22.	A
23.	A
24.	D
25.	B

TEST 2

DIRECTIONS: Each question or incomplete statement is followed by several suggested answers or completions. Select the one that BEST answers the question or completes the statement. *PRINT THE LETTER OF THE CORRECT ANSWER IN THE SPACE AT THE RIGHT.*

1. In which one of the following pairs do the two rocks MOST closely resemble each other in appearance?

    A. Basalt and granite   B. Granite and pegmatite
    C. Conglomerate and sandstone   D. Felsite and scoria

1____

2. A goniometer is used to measure

    A. crystal angles   B. crystal displacement
    C. glacial movement   D. upper wind velocities

2____

3. The bedrock on Manhattan Island is, for the MOST part,

    A. granite   B. schist   C. sandstone   D. gneiss

3____

4. Geodes are MOST commonly found in which one of the following?

    A. Granite   B. Limestone   C. Sandstone   D. Shale

4____

5. Foliation is associated with the class of rocks known as

    A. igneous   B. sedimentary
    C. metamorphic   D. fossiliferous

5____

6. The cap rock of Niagara Falls is a massive layer of

    A. basalt   B. limestone   C. sandstone   D. shale

6____

7. Loess is a fine-grained sedimentary rock deposited by

    A. precipitation from water solutions
    B. continental glaciers
    C. slow-flowing streams
    D. wind action

7____

8. The Sierra Nevada Mountains were formed PRINCIPALLY by

    A. folding   B. block faulting
    C. thrust faulting   D. glaciation

8____

9. A shallow horseshoe-shaped lake was PROBABLY formed as a result of

    A. an earthquake   B. glaciation
    C. river action   D. a volcanic eruption

9____

10. Sink holes occur PRINCIPALLY in regions whose bedrock is

    A. granite   B. limestone   C. schist   D. sandstone

10____

11. Abandoned iron mines in the Adirondack Mountains of New York have recently been re-opened for the recovery of   11____

    A. manganese   B. titanium   C. antimony   D. strontium

12. A metamorphic rock composed PRINCIPALLY of the mineral calcite is   12____

    A. gneiss   B. marble   C. schist   D. slate

13. A pair of minerals ALWAYS found in granites is   13____

    A. augite and magnetite   B. calcite and mica
    C. feldspar and quartz   D. hornblende and talc

14. Within the confines of Greater New York, rock deposited in the Age of the Dinosaurs is   14____

    A. a sandstone on Staten Island
    B. gneiss in the Bronx
    C. marble beneath the East River
    D. schist in Central Park

15. The mineral MOST resistant to both chemical and mechanical weathering is   15____

    A. calcite   B. hornblende   C. feldspar   D. quartz

16. At the end of 11,000 years, the percentage of carbon-14 that will be found in an artifact is CLOSEST to which one of the following?   16____

    A. 10%   B. 18%   C. 25%   D. 50%

17. Instead of a Geiger tube, the scintillation counter contains a crystal of   17____

    A. zinc sulphate   B. uranium oxide
    C. sodium carbonate   D. sodium iodide

18. Which one of the following pairs includes a metamorphic rock and the rock from which it was derived?   18____

    A. Slate, limestone   B. Granite, shale
    C. Obsidian, marble   D. Sandstone, quartzite

19. When feldspar decomposes, it forms the mineral   19____

    A. flint   B. kaolinite   C. hornblende   D. talc

20. Plaster of Paris is made from the mineral   20____

    A. gypsum   B. anhydrite   C. aragonite   D. calcite

21. Of the following minerals, the one that has been MOST often used in the manufacture of phosphate-rich fertilizers is   21____

    A. kaolinite   B. feldspar   C. apatite   D. fluorite

22. The chemical composition of the mineral pyrite is   22____

    A. $FeCO_3$ B. $AuTe_2$ C. FeS_2 D. Fe_2O_3

23. The MOST porous rock among the following is 23____

    A. slate   B. quartzite   C. basalt   D. conglomerate

24. Of the following rocks, the one that will NOT effervesce in cold dilute hydrochloric acid is   24____

    A. basalt   B. marble   C. limestone   D. chalk

25. Of the following rocks, the one that cooled MOST slowly from the molten state was 25____

    A. obsidian   B. gabbro   C. basalt   D. felsite

_____

KEY (CORRECT ANSWERS)

1.	B		11.	B
2.	A		12.	B
3.	B		13.	C
4.	B		14.	A
5.	C		15.	D
6.	B		16.	C
7.	D		17.	D
8.	B		18.	D
9.	C		19.	B
10.	B		20.	A

21.	C
22.	C
23.	D
24.	A
25.	B

_____

TEST 3

DIRECTIONS: Each question or incomplete statement is followed by several suggested answers or completions. Select the one that BEST answers the question or completes the statement. *PRINT THE LETTER OF THE CORRECT ANSWER IN THE SPACE AT THE RIGHT.*

1. Of the following, the bedrock of a karst region is MOST likely to be   1____

   A. granite   B. sandstone   C. limestone   D. shale

2. Of the following rocks, the one that contains visible crystals of feldspar is   2____

   A. granite   B. marble   C. sandstone   D. shale

3. The BEST evidence for a past period of arid climate is an extensive deposit of which one of the following?   3____

   A. Limestone   B. Salt   C. Shale   D. Glacial till

4. Among the following substances, the SOFTEST is   4____

   A. topaz   B. quartz   C. feldspar   D. calcite

5. Of the following, the MOST reliable estimates of the age of the earth are obtained by a study of   5____

   A. index fossils
   B. radioactive minerals
   C. the salt content of the oceans
   D. the thickness of sedimentary rocks

6. The size of crystals of an igneous rock is determined PRIMARILY by its   6____

   A. chemical composition   B. rate of cooling
   C. specific gravity   D. acidity

7. Among the following, the bedrock MOST rapidly destroyed by ground water is   7____

   A. schist   B. sandstone   C. limestone   D. gneiss

8. Wind deposits of unstratified, yellowish silt are called   8____

   A. loess   B. mantle   C. talus   D. creep

9. Fossils are MOST likely to be found in rocks that are classified as   9____

   A. igneous   B. sedimentary   C. metamorphic   D. granitic

10. On the Mohs' scale of hardness, a penny has a hardness that is CLOSEST to which one of the following?   10____

    A. 1   B. 3   C. 5   D. 7

11. Of the following types of igneous intrusion, the one that commonly forms the core of mountain ranges is called a   11____

    A. dike   B. sill   C. laccolith   D. batholith

12. Of the following, the mineral group MOST resistant to weathering is   12____

    A. feldspar   B. mica   C. quartz   D. amphibole

13. Among the following minerals, the one that will effervesce with cold dilute hydrochloric   13____
acid is

    A. selenite   B. calcite   C. fluorite   D. brotite

14. The soapstone used as the acid-resistant top of chemistry laboratory tables is made   14____
PRINCIPALLY of

    A. talc   B. andesite   C. rhyolite   D. peridotite

15. Limestone is to marble as shale is to   15____

    A. sandstone   B. slate   C. granite   D. gneiss

16. Of the following substances, the one which BEST shows conchoidal fracture is   16____

    A. galena   B. granite   C. mica   D. obsidian

17. Fossils are MOST likely to be found in which one of the following?   17____

    A. Granite   B. Gneiss   C. Obsidian   D. Shale

18. Iron is obtained from which one of the following?   18____

    A. Bauxite   B. Galena   C. Hematite   D. Chalcopyrite

19. The material commonly used for streak plates in mineral testing is   19____

    A. glass   B. porcelain   C. slate   D. steel

20. Which one of the following characterizes scoria, basalt, pumice, and obsidian?   20____

    A. Dark color   B. Large crystals
    C. Igneous   D. Glassy

21. The MOST common metallic element in the earth's crust is which one of the following?   21____

    A. Silicon   B. Iron   C. Copper   D. Aluminum

22. Fossils are found MOST frequently in   22____

    A. clay   B. sandstone   C. granite   D. basalt

23. Rocks transported and deposited elsewhere by glacial action are called   23____

    A. striae   B. drumlins
    C. Roches mountonnées   D. erratics

24. The metamorphic rock formed when pure limestone is recrystallized is   24____

    A. gneiss   B. marble   C. schist   D. slate

25. The one of the following which is the basis for the MOST accurate method of determining   25____
the age of rocks is

    A. index fossils   B. rate of decomposition
    C. radioactivity   D. none of these

KEY (CORRECT ANSWERS)

1.	C	11.	D
2.	A	12.	C
3.	B	13.	B
4.	D	14.	A
5.	B	15.	B
6.	B	16.	D
7.	C	17.	D
8.	A	18.	C
9.	B	19.	B
10.	B	20.	C

21.	D
22.	B
23.	D
24.	B
25.	C

TEST 4

DIRECTIONS: Each question or incomplete statement is followed by several suggested answers or completions. Select the one that BEST answers the question or completes the statement. *PRINT THE LETTER OF THE CORRECT ANSWER IN THE SPACE AT THE RIGHT.*

1. Of the following, the rock which is NOT affected to a great extent by chemical erosion is   1____

   A. calcite   B. marble   C. sandstone   D. limestone

2. A lobster-like invertebrate, the trilobite, was the MOST dominant form of life during the   2____
   _____ era.

   A. Archeozoic   B. Proterozoic
   C. Paleozoic   D. Mesozoic

3. Modern theory concerning the causes of an ice age asserts that man may inadvertently   3____
   trigger another ice age by

   A. breaking up the ice in the Arctic Sea
   B. seeding clouds
   C. exploding an H-bomb in the Van Allen belt
   D. none of the above

4. The *Tsunami* result from   4____

   A. earthquakes   B. hurricanes
   C. tornadoes   D. violent thunderstorms

5. The igneous intrusion composing the Palisades of the Hudson is a   5____

   A. laccolith   B. dike
   C. sill   D. none of the above

6. The Black Hills of South Dakota are examples of   6____

   A. dome mountains   B. block mountains
   C. volcanic mountains   D. none of the above

7. Caverns are LEAST likely to form in regions underlain by which one of the following?   7____

   A. Limestone   B. Gypsum   C. Rock salt   D. Sandstone

8. Of the following rock samples, the one which bubbles when treated with hydrochloric acid   8____
   is

   A. granite   B. sandstone   C. limestone   D. sphalerite

9. Fossils are MOST likely to be found in which one of the following?   9____

   A. Gneiss   B. Shale   C. Obsidian   D. Felsite

10. In which one of the following types of rocks is oil found in oil fields?   10____

    A. Aeolian   B. Metamorphic   C. Igneous   D. Sedimentary

11. Quartz belongs to the crystal system known as   11____

    A. isometric   B. hexagonal   C. monoclinic   D. orthorhombic

12. Of the following minerals, the one MOST abundant in the earth's crust is   12____

    A. feldspar   B. quartz   C. hornblende   D. mica

13. Of the following, the mineral MOST abundant in stony meteorites is   13____

    A. calcite   B. muscovite   C. olivine   D. quartz

14. Of the following, the division of geologic time in which the MOST extensive glaciation occurred in the Southern Hemisphere is the   14____

    A. Jurassic   B. Permian   C. Pleistocene   D. Silurian

15. Of the following, the HARDEST mineral is   15____

    A. apatite   B. fluorite   C. quartz   D. topaz

16. Which one of the following forms of coal has been MOST changed from the original vegetation?   16____

    A. Anthracite   B. Bituminous   C. Lignite   D. Peat

17. Which one of the following fossiliferous organisms is a plant?   17____

    A. Crinoid   B. Diatom   C. Foraminifera   D. Radiolaria

18. Using P for Permian epoch, C for Cambrian epoch, M for Miocene epoch, E for Eocene epoch, which one of the following is the CORRECT sequence going from the oldest to the most recent epoch?   18____

    A. P,C,M,E   B. M,E,P,C   C. C,P,E,M   D. E,M,C,P

19. Which one of the following is a mineral that separates very easily into thin elastic sheets?   19____

    A. Mica   B. Malachite   C. Calcite   D. Quartz

20. A rock specimen, hollow on the inside and partially filled with quartz crystals, is called a   20____

    A. geode   B. neve   C. travertine   D. gabbro

21. Cinnabar is an ore of   21____

    A. mercury   B. tin   C. uranium   D. zinc

22. On the Mohs' scale, a steel pocketknife has a hardness CLOSEST to which one of the following?   22____

    A. 3.5   B. 4.5   C. 5.5   D. 6.5

23. If a mineral specimen weighs 10 grams in air, and when immersed in water appears to weight 7 grams, then the specific gravity of the specimen is   23____

    A. 7/10   B. 1 3/7   C. 2 1/3   D. 3 1/3

24. Of the following, which rock is NOT a sedimentary rock?   24____

    A. Gneiss   B. Limestone   C. Shale   D. Sandstone

25. A geologic feature NOT characteristic of a region that was covered by alpine glaciers is a   25____

   A. hanging valley   B. v-shaped valley
   C. cirque   D. tarn

KEY (CORRECT ANSWERS)

1.	C		11.	B
2.	C		12.	A
3.	A		13.	C
4.	A		14.	B
5.	C		15.	D
6.	A		16.	A
7.	D		17.	B
8.	C		18.	C
9.	B		19.	A
10.	D		20.	A

21.	A
22.	C
23.	D
24.	A
25.	B

TEST 5

DIRECTIONS: Each question or incomplete statement is followed by several suggested answers or completions. Select the one that BEST answers the question or completes the statement. *PRINT THE LETTER OF THE CORRECT ANSWER IN THE SPACE AT THE RIGHT.*

1. Of the following ratios, the one which would NOT be useful as the basis for a method of dating igenous rocks over 1,000,000 years old is

   A. Uranium 238 / Lead 206
   B. Rubidium 87 / Strontium 87
   C. Carbon 14 / Carbon 12
   D. Potassium 40 / Argon 40

   1____

2. Fossil evidence has indisputably shown that the origin of the camel was in which one of the following regions?

   A. Indo-China   B. Egypt
   C. Australia   D. North America

   2____

3. Carbonized fossils MOST frequently represent evidence of which one of the following forms of life?

   A. Plants   B. Trilobites   C. Brachiopods   D. Corals

   3____

4. Of the following, the CHIEF product of chemical weathering is

   A. clay   B. feldspar   C. mica   D. slate

   4____

5. Of the following, the ONLY group that includes one igneous rock, one sedimentary rock, and one metamorphic rock is

   A. arkose, gabbro, quartzite
   B. andesite, basalt, conglomerate
   C. gneiss, marble, shale
   D. limestone, phyllite, schist

   5____

6. Of the following, the mineral that is the MOST likely source of kaolin, after weathering, is

   A. calcite   B. feldspar   C. magnetite   D. quartz

   6____

7. Of the following, which one is a light spongy rock?

   A. Obsidian   B. Basalt   C. Talus   D. Pumice

   7____

8. Which one of the following terms is NOT a process involving chemical decomposition in rocks?

   A. Exfoliation   B. Hydrolysis
   C. Hydration   D. Oxidation

   8____

9. Which one of the following will react with dilute hydrochloric acid?

   A. Travertine   B. Kaolin   C. Garnet   D. Gypsum

   9____

10. Which one of the following rocks is MOST easily weathered by freezing and thawing?   10____

    A. Sandstone   B. Obsidian   C. Pegmatite   D. Basalt

11. The bedrock which is MOST widespread in New York City is   11____

    A. mica schist   B. gneiss   C. dolomite   D. granite

12. In which one of the following regions is bauxite mined?   12____

    A. Franklin Furnace, New Jersey
    B. Little Rock, Arkansas
    C. Birmingham, Alabama
    D. Bisbee, Arizona

13. Which one of the following minerals can be scratched by a fingernail?   13____

    A. Selenite   B. Apatite   C. Feldspar   D. Corundum

14. When water and carbon dioxide act on limestone rock to dissolve it, the soluble substance formed has the formula   14____

    A. $CaCO_3$ B. $CaHCO_3$ C. $Ca(HCO_3)_2$ D. $CaSO_4$

15. The presence of which one of the following produces a pink variety of granite?   15____

    A. Quartz   B. Feldspar   C. Mica   D. Hornblende

16. Sedimentary rock is forming MOST rapidly today in the   16____

    A. St. Lawrence River Valley
    B. Pacific Coast of North America
    C. Grand Canyon
    D. Gulf of Mexico

17. The progress of scientific petrology was accelerated by microscopic inspection using   17____

    A. better staining agents
    B. polarized light
    C. uniform sections
    D. infra-red portion of spectrum

18. Functioning artesian wells may be found when an aquifer occurs between layers of   18____

    A. shale   B. sandstone   C. conglomerate   D. pumice

19. Which one of the following types of fossil organisms has a short life span and worldwide distribution?   19____

    A. Fossil assemblages   B. Fossil species
    C. Index fossils   D. Historical fossils

20. In which one of the following are fossils LEAST likely to be found?   20____

    A. Aeolian sediments   B. Marine sediments
    C. Continental sediments   D. Intrusive igneous rocks

21. Which one of the following is especially important in identifying oil horizons?　　21____

    A. Foraminifera   B. Diatoms
    C. Radiolaria   D. Graptolites

22. Which one of the following groups BEST describes ostraco-derms?　　22____

    A. Primitive, bony, possessing lungs
    B. Primitive, jawless, armored
    C. Ray-finned, fan-tailed
    D. Lobe-finned with only a fringe of true fin

23. The age, in years, of the oldest rocks from which records of geologic history have been decipered in considerable detail is CLOSEST to which one of the following?　　23____

    A. 200 million   B. 500 million
    C. 1.5 billion   D. 3.0 billion

24. The fine clay found at the top of a varve representing one year of deposition is formed during which one of the following seasons?　　24____

    A. Winter   B. Spring   C. Summer   D. Autumn

25. Of the following, which one left the POOREST fossil record?　　25____

    A. Echinodermata   B. Annelida
    C. Mollusca   D. Brachiopoda

KEY (CORRECT ANSWERS)

1.	C		11.	A
2.	D		12.	B
3.	A		13.	A
4.	A		14.	C
5.	A		15.	B
6.	B		16.	D
7.	D		17.	B
8.	A		18.	A
9.	A		19.	C
10.	A		20.	D

21.	A
22.	B
23.	B
24.	A
25.	B

EXAMINATION SECTION
TEST 1

DIRECTIONS: Each question or incomplete statement is followed by several suggested answers or completions. Select the one that BEST answers the question or completes the statement. *PRINT THE LETTER OF THE CORRECT ANSWER IN THE SPACE AT THE RIGHT.*

1. Which one of the following types of coal was formed LARGELY from windblown spores and pollen?　　1.＿＿

    A. Lignite   B. Cannel   C. Bituminous   D. Anthracite

2. Which one of the following kinds of fuels has the HIGHEST heat value?　　2.＿＿

    A. Anthracite   B. Bituminous   C. Lignite   D. Peat

3. Which one of the following elements in the earth's crust is the MOST abundant?　　3.＿＿

    A. Titanium   B. Hydrogen   C. Sulphur   D. Carbon

4. In which one of the following countries are the LARGEST known reserves of mercury ore located?　　4.＿＿

    A. Spain   B. United States   C. Mexico   D. Italy

5. The United States relies ALMOST entirely on imports for its supply of　　5.＿＿

    A. silver   B. aluminum   C. tin   D. lead

6. Of the following, the rock MOST likely to serve as an aquifer is　　6.＿＿

    A. basalt   B. granite   C. quartzite   D. sandstone

7. Of the following, an important ore of titanium is the mineral　　7.＿＿

    A. stibnite   B. rutile   C. realgar   D. scheelite

8. Which one of the following countries is the LARGEST producer of nickel ore?　　8.＿＿

    A. New Caledonia   B. United States
    C. Russia   D. Canada

9. Of the following, which one is the PRINCIPAL factor responsible for contact metamorphism?　　9.＿＿

    A. Confining pressure
    B. Shearing stress
    C. Temperature
    D. Lack of chemical equilibrium

10. Of the following properties, the one common to chalk, diatomite, kaolin, and talc is　　10.＿＿

    A. same chemical composition
    B. overall hardness less than 2
    C. effervescence with dilute HCl
    D. their classification as minerals

11. A xenolith is a   11.____

    A. cavity in sedimentary rocks lined with crystals
    B. cavity left in lava by escaping gases
    C. form of igneous intrusion
    D. fragment of country rock enclosed in an igneous intrusion

12. Of the following, an example of a *simple oxide* occurring in nature is the mineral   12.____

    A. hematite   B. muscovite   C. labradorite   D. calcite

13. Perthite is a(n)   13.____

    A. homogeneous mineral
    B. intimate intergrowth between quartz and orthoclase
    C. intimate intergrowth between two types of feldspar
    D. type of volcanic glass

14. Of the following, the geologic measurement which can be applied ONLY to folds is   14.____

    A. strike   B. plunge   C. rake   D. dip

15. Of the following, an example of a clastic or detrital sedimentary rock is   15.____

    A. coal   B. coral limestone
    C. siltstone   D. gypsum rock

16. The expression *streak* of a mineral   16.____

    A. refers to its luster
    B. is its overall color
    C. is a measure of its brittleness
    D. refers to the color of its powder

17. Of the following rocks, the one having the LOWEST density is   17.____

    A. basalt   B. obsidian   C. pumice   D. granite

18. Of the following, the one in which fossils are NEVER found is   18.____

    A. asphalt   B. slate   C. amber   D. ice

19. Sedimentary rocks of the Cretaceous and Tertiary ages are PRINCIPALLY found in the Physiographic Province known as the   19.____

    A. Appalachian Plateau   B. Folded Appalachians
    C. New England Upland   D. Atlantic Coastal Plain

20. Of the following, the example of an epoch in the geologic time scale is the   20.____

    A. Mesozoic   B. Permian   C. Mississippian   D. Pliocene

21. Which of the following events marks the beginning of geologic time?   21.____

    A. Formation of the first igneous rock
    B. Formation of the first sedimentary rock
    C. Preservation of the first fossils
    D. First appearance of man on earth

22. Archaeopteryx, a flying animal of the Mesozoic world, belonged to the phylum   22._____

    A. Reptilia   B. Amphibia   C. Aves   D. Mammalia

23. The approximate percentage of geologic time represented by the Pre-Cambrian Era is   23._____

    A. 20%   B. 40%   C. 60%   D. 80%

24. The use of igneous rocks in establishing the geologic time scale depends upon the fact   24._____
that they

    A. have a great diversity of composition
    B. usually contain fossils
    C. have invaded earlier rocks of known age
    D. often contain appreciable quantities of radioactive minerals

25. Foraminifera are primitive   25._____

    A. single-celled plants
    B. multi-celled invertebrates
    C. single-celled invertebrates
    D. vertebrates

KEY (CORRECT ANSWERS)

1. B		11. D	
2. A		12. A	
3. A		13. C	
4. A		14. B	
5. C		15. C	
6. D		16. D	
7. B		17. C	
8. D		18. B	
9. C		19. D	
10. B		20. D	

21. B
22. C
23. D
24. D
25. C

TEST 2

DIRECTIONS: Each question or incomplete statement is followed by several suggested answers or completions. Select the one that BEST answers the question or completes the statement. *PRINT THE LETTER OF THE CORRECT ANSWER IN THE SPACE AT THE RIGHT.*

1. The type of solid fuel MOST likely to be found in strata which were deeply buried, but not folded, is   1.____

   A. bituminous coal   B. lignite
   C. anthracite   D. peat

2. Of the following, the mineral with a SINGLE perfect cleavage is   2.____

   A. calcite   B. magnetite   C. muscovite   D. hornblende

3. The PRINCIPAL ore of aluminum is the mineral   3.____

   A. bauxite   B. bornite   C. celestite   D. cerussite

4. A common ore of lead is   4.____

   A. magnetite   B. galena   C. pyrite   D. sphalerite

5. Emerald is a gem variety of the mineral   5.____

   A. garnet   B. tourmaline   C. beryl   D. corundum

6. The end-product of the chemical weathering of feldspar is likely to be   6.____

   A. kaolin   B. quartz   C. calcite   D. gypsum

7. An igneous rock composed of 60% feldspar, 30% quartz, and 10% hornblende having an even-grained texture is   7.____

   A. basalt   B. gabbro   C. granite   D. diorite

8. A MOST important feature of distinction between a sandstone and a conglomerate is   8.____

   A. color   B. texture   C. hardness   D. composition

9. Underground streams are commonly found in regions underlain by   9.____

   A. shale   B. granite   C. sandstone   D. limestone

10. Taconite is an important reserve source of   10.____

    A. coal   B. copper   C. iron   D. phosphates

11. The mineral wolframite is an important source of the element   11.____

    A. osmium   B. tantalum   C. titanium   D. tungsten

12. The mineral whose presence in solution is MOST frequently the cause of hardness in water is   12.____

    A. calcite   B. feldspar   C. mica   D. quartz

13. Which one of the following does NOT occur as a *native element*? 13.____

    A. Carbon   B. Zinc   C. Sulfur   D. Copper

14. The mineral dolomite contains 14.____

    A. calcium and iron   B. magnesium and aluminum
    C. potassium and sodium   D. calcium and magnesium

15. An element present in orthoclase feldspars but NOT in plagioclase feldspars is 15.____

    A. Al   B. Ca   C. K   D. Na

16. The spectacular development and subsequent extinction of the dinosaurs occurred during the geologic era called 16.____

    A. Pre-Cambrian   B. Cenozoic   C. Mesozoic   D. Paleozoic

17. The MOST abundant metal in the earth's crust is 17.____

    A. aluminum   B. iron   C. lead   D. copper

18. The PRINCIPAL anthracite coal deposits of the United States occur in the 18.____

    A. Appalachian Plateau   B. Atlantic Coastal Plain
    C. Folded Appalachians   D. Piedmont Province

19. Bisbee, Arizona, is MOST famous as a mining center for 19.____

    A. copper   B. gold   C. iron   D. lead

20. The rock which MOST commonly forms the aquifer of an artesian formation is 20.____

    A. conglomerate   B. limestone   C. sandstone   D. shale

21. Cleavage is possible because of 21.____

    A. weaknesses in the atomic structure of minerals
    B. perfectly balanced valence forces
    C. kinetic metamorphism of rocks
    D. mechanical weathering of minerals

22. Of the following, the rock which cooled MOST slowly from a molten state is 22.____

    A. granite   B. pumice   C. marble   D. basalt

23. A soft, white rock composed of the calcareous shells of microscopic animals is 23.____

    A. kaolin   B. diatomaceous earth
    C. soapstone   D. chalk

24. An example of a fine grained, clastic sedimentary rock is 24.____

    A. limestone   B. gypsum   C. shale   D. pumice

25. Ruby is a gem variety of the mineral 25.____

    A. garnet   B. quartz   C. tourmaline   D. corundum

KEY (CORRECT ANSWERS)

1.	A	11.	D
2.	C	12.	A
3.	A	13.	B
4.	B	14.	D
5.	C	15.	C
6.	A	16.	C
7.	C	17.	A
8.	B	18.	C
9.	D	19.	A
10.	C	20.	C

21.	A
22.	A
23.	D
24.	C
25.	D

TEST 3

DIRECTIONS: Each question or incomplete statement is followed by several suggested answers or completions. Select the one that BEST answers the question or completes the statement. *PRINT THE LETTER OF THE CORRECT ANSWER IN THE SPACE AT THE RIGHT.*

1. A common ore of zinc is the mineral   1.____

   A. ilmenite   B. sphalerite   C. pyrite   D. carnotite

2. Dense or aphanitic textures are characteristic of igneous rocks which are   2.____

   A. intrusive
   B. light-colored and relatively lightweight
   C. extrusive
   D. dark-colored and relatively heavy

3. The contraction theory was formulated to explain the origin of forces which caused the   3.____

   A. rise of the sea level following the last Ice Age
   B. steady rise of the north shore of the Baltic Sea
   C. folding of the rocks in New York City
   D. elevation of marine terraces along the coast of California

4. Of the following, the one that is NOT a uranium ore is   4.____

   A. autunite   B. carnotite   C. gummite   D. bornite

5. One variety of talc is known as   5.____

   A. enargite   B. pitchstone   C. selenite   D. soapstone

6. A variety of sandstone that is flexible is   6.____

   A. alunite   B. itacolumite   C. kyanite   D. specularite

7. The rock whose mineral content MOST strongly resembles that of granite is   7.____

   A. andesite   B. rhyolite   C. periodotite   D. trachyte

8. A common variety of pyroxene is the mineral   8.____

   A. augite   B. beryl   C. albite   D. olivine

9. The iron ores of the Lake Superior region of the United States occur in rocks whose age   9.____
   is dated as

   A. Cenozoic   B. Mesozoic   C. Paleozoic   D. Proterozoic

10. The physiographic plateau which leads in the production of uranium ore in the United   10.____
    States is the

    A. Appalachian   B. Colorado   C. Columbia   D. Ozark

11. The oldest rock which outcrops in New York City and vicinity is   11.____

    A. Manhattan schist   B. Inwood marble
    C. Fordham gneiss   D. Palisades diabase

115

12. The olivine zone in the Palisades resulted from   12.____

    A. the intrusion of a sill within a sill
    B. metamorphism of part of the sill
    C. gravitational settling of early crystals
    D. slower cooling in the center of the sill

13. The contact between the Newark series and the New York City rocks beneath the Hudson River is a(n)   13.____

    A. normal fault
    B. conformable sedimentary contact
    C. reverse fault
    D. unconformable sedimentary contact

14. The MOST plausible explanation for our failure to find fossils in the rocks underlying the Boroughs of Manhattan and the Bronx is that   14.____

    A. there are too few exposures of these rocks to permit adequate study
    B. the glaciers of the last Ice Age removed the fossil-bearing strata
    C. little or no organic life existed at the time of their formation
    D. metamorphism has obscured or destroyed probable fossil evidence in sedimentary rocks

15. Baluchitherium is the name given by paleontologists to the   15.____

    A. carnivorous flying dinosaur
    B. prehistoric apeman discovered in Tibet
    C. giant shark of Devonian time
    D. largest land mammal ever known

16. Salt deposits in central New York State near Syracuse were formed during the geologic period called the   16.____

    A. Cambrian   B. Miocene   C. Silurian   D. Triassic

17. The LARGEST subdivision of the geologic time scale in terms of elapsed years is a(n)   17.____

    A. epoch   B. period   C. era   D. age

18. Crossopterygians are notable in earth history as   18.____

    A. an early species of dinosaur
    B. primitive seed plants of Mississippian time
    C. ancestors of the first amphibians
    D. a link between reptiles and mammals

19. Of the following, the mountains of GREATEST geologic age are the   19.____

    A. Appalachians   B. Rockies
    C. Sierra Nevadas   D. Cascades

20. Laccoliths are found in   20.____

    A. domed mountains   B. block mountains
    C. folded mountains   D. volcanoes

21. The normal percentage of dissolved mineral matter in sea water (by weight) is APPROX- 21.____
    IMATELY

    A. 1.5   B. 2.5   C. 3.5   D. 4.5

22. A shoreline formed as a result of submergence is a shoreline   22.____

    A. coastal plain   B. delta
    C. fiord   D. volcano

23. The Palisades of New Jersey originated as an igneous intrusion during the period known   23.____
    as

    A. Eocene   B. Cretaceous   C. Permian   D. Triassic

24. An outstanding example of a glacial trough is the   24.____

    A. Grand Canyon of the Colorado
    B. Yellowstone Canyon in Yellowstone National Park
    C. Yosemite Valley in Yosemite National Park
    D. Zion Canyon in Zion National Park

25. A xenolith is a   25.____

    A. cavity in sedimentary rocks lined with crystals
    B. cavity left in lava by escaping gases
    C. form of igneous intrusion
    D. fragment of country rock enclosed in an igneous intrusion

KEY (CORRECT ANSWERS)

1.	B		11.	C
2.	C		12.	C
3.	C		13.	D
4.	D		14.	D
5.	D		15.	D
6.	B		16.	C
7.	B		17.	C
8.	A		18.	C
9.	D		19.	A
10.	B		20.	A

21.	C
22.	C
23.	D
24.	C
25.	D

TEST 4

DIRECTIONS: Each question or incomplete statement is followed by several suggested answers or completions. Select the one that BEST answers the question or completes the statement. *PRINT THE LETTER OF THE CORRECT ANSWER IN THE SPACE AT THE RIGHT.*

1. The Keewatin Glacier of the Pleistocene ice age was centered in   1.____

    A. north central Canada   B. Labrador
    C. Alaska   D. Greenland

2. The Royal Gorge of the Arkansas River represents a river valley which is   2.____

    A. young   B. mature   C. old   D. subdued

3. Sink holes are the result of the work of   3.____

    A. earthquakes   B. underground water
    C. streams   D. glaciers

4. A river is classified as mature when it includes a   4.____

    A. chain of lakes in its course
    B. gorge
    C. series of meanders
    D. series of rapids

5. An esker is a   5.____

    A. winding, roughly stratified glacial ridge
    B. linear, unstratified glacial ridge
    C. roughly circular glacial mound
    D. series of glacial elevations and depressions

6. An example of an active volcano of the *quiet* type is   6.____

    A. Krakatoa   B. Mauna Loa
    C. Mt. Lassen   D. Mt. Vesuvius

7. Stone Mt., Georgia, is classified as a   7.____

    A. butte   B. mesa
    C. monadnock   D. volcanic neck

8. A rock composed of angular fragments cemented together into a coherent mass is a   8.____

    A. breccia   B. tufa   C. conglomerate   D. dacite

9. In Moh's scale of mineral hardness, quartz is number   9.____

    A. 5   B. 6   C. 7   D. 8

10. A rock which shows foliated structure is   10.____

    A. marble   B. serpentine   C. schist   D. quartzite

11. The LATEST of the geological eras is called the

    A. cenozoic   B. paleozoic   C. proterozoic   D. mesozoic

11.____

12. The mineral which is LEAST susceptible to chemical weathering is

    A. feldspar   B. hornblends   C. augite   D. quartz

12.____

13. An animal that is PROBABLY a link between the fish and amphibia is the

    A. archeopteryx   B. coelacanth
    C. trilobite   D. lamprey

13.____

14. Lost rivers or underground streams are MOST likely to occur in regions whose bedrock is

    A. limestone   B. slate   C. granite   D. conglomerate

14.____

15. The commonest cause of hard water is the presence of compounds of

    A. fluorine   B. calcium   C. iron   D. sulfur

15.____

16. All of the following metals are extracted from the minerals with which they are associated below EXCEPT

    A. iron from hematite   B. uranium from pitchblende
    C. tin from sphalerite   D. lead from galena

16.____

17. Iron pyrites, sometimes known as fool's gold, is mined CHIEFLY for use in the manufacture of

    A. costume jewelry   B. sulfuric acid
    C. porcelain and china   D. paint

17.____

18. Of the following groups, the one which contains ONLY metamorphic rocks is

    A. basalt, diorite, dolomite, shale
    B. conglomerate, granite, serpentine, marble
    C. diabase, schist, obsidian, serpentine
    D. quartzite, gneiss, slate, marble

18.____

19. Of the following groups of materials found in the earth's crust, the group in which the items range progressively from softest to hardest is

    A. talc, fluorite, quartz, diamond
    B. feldspar, gypsum, topaz, corundum
    C. gypsum, quartz, apatite, diamond
    D. calcite, quartz, diamond, corundum

19.____

20. Of the following acids, the one MOST often used to test for calcite is cold dilute _____ acid.

    A. hydrochloric   B. carbonic
    C. sulfuric   D. nitric

20.____

21. The destructive distillation of soft coal produces

    A. coal gas, bitumen, water gas, and tar
    B. ammonia, coal gas, water gas, and coke

21.____

C. coal tar, coal gas, ammonia, and coke
D. coal tar, coke, ammonia, and charcoal

22. The bedrock of a large part of New York County is the rock called 22.____

   A. granite   B. quartzite   C. schist   D. trap

23. When in New York City (which is at longitude 75°W), it is 9:00 A.M., real time February 23.____
    22. In Calcutta (90°E longitude), the real time is which one of the following?

   A. 8:00 P.M., February 22   B. 8:00 A.M., February 21
   C. 8:00 P.M., February 23   D. 8:00 A.M., February 22

24. The length, in miles, of a degree of longitude at a latitude of 60° is CLOSEST to which 24.____
    one of the following?

   A. 18   B. 27   C. 35   D. 60

25. Which one of the following is a natural water softener frequently used in the laboratory? 25.____

   A. Activated charcoal   B. Sodium Zeolite
   C. Sodium silicate   D. Alum

_____

KEY (CORRECT ANSWERS)

1.	A	11.	A
2.	A	12.	D
3.	B	13.	B
4.	D	14.	A
5.	A	15.	B
6.	B	16.	C
7.	C	17.	B
8.	A	18.	D
9.	C	19.	A
10.	C	20.	A

21.	C
22.	C
23.	A
24.	C
25.	B

_____

BASIC FUNDAMENTALS OF GEOLOGY, GEOPHYSICS AND EARTH SCIENCE

CONTENTS

			Page
CHAPTER-	I.	THE DEVELOPMENT OF THE EARTH	1
	II.	INSIDE THE EARTH	6
	III.	ROCKS AND MINERALS	12
	IV.	CHANGING THE FACE OF THE EARTH	17
	V.	GLACIERS	21
	VI.	PRESSURE INSIDE THE EARTH	25
	VII.	VOLCANOES	29

BASIC FUNDAMENTALS OF GEOLOGY, GEOPHYSICS AND EARTH SCIENCE

CHAPTER I. THE DEVELOPMENT OF THE EARTH

According to recent estimates, the earth is over four billion years old. Of course, these estimates may be wrong, but we can say that probably the earth is at least four billion years old.

For millions of years the earth has been part of the solar system. What was happening here during all this time? This is the question that *historical geologists* try to answer. In this unit we will see what they have been able to learn about the early part of this planet's history. You will notice that there is no mention of man on earth until fairly recently. That is because man has been on earth only about a million years. Our actual records of people go back only a few thousand years. This is only a tiny part of the earth's history.

How Geologists Work

Most of our knowledge of the early history of the earth comes from records preserved in solid rock. From time to time some living plant or animal died and left its imprint in rock. The print was preserved for millions of years. These records of living things are called *fossils*.

In some fossils the rock has preserved many of the details of the plants or animals, such as the scales of fish or the veins in tree leaves. Some of the fossils found in hard coal, for example, show ferns that grew when the coal was first started millions of years ago.

Sometimes we find actual remains of plants and animals that have been preserved by nature for thousands of years. An insect or a leaf may get caught in the gummy resin that comes from trees. If the gum completely covers the insect or plant parts, they can be preserved intact for thousands of years in the hardened tree gum. Geologists sorietimes find the bodies of whole insects trapped in this way. But this type of fossil is usually not very old in geological terms. The geologist is interested in fossils that are millions - not just thousands - of years old. The bones of animals and the leaves of plants cannot last more than a few thousand years. But a print in rock can last indefinitely. So our oldest fossils are found in solid rock.

Sometimes, too, complete animals have been found preserved in ice for some thousands of years. About twenty-thousand years ago an animal that looked like a large elephant lived on earth. We call it the *hairy mammoth*. Several of these mammoths have been found preserved in solid ice. Only a few years ago in northern Russia one of these animals was found perfectly preserved in an ice block. But information of this sort does not help the geologist in his study of the earth's very distant past. It is not old enough.

Some of the strangest fossils ever found are the trees and plants that have "turned to stone." We say that they have been *petrified*. There are a good many of these stone trees in the United States. Actually the tree does not turn to stone. When the dead tree takes in water, it also takes in minerals in the water. The water evaporates, but the hard mineral is left as a rocky deposit. It actually takes the shape of the cells in the tree and fills them. When the cells waste away, the solid rock is left. The tree is like a mold which has been filled with rock particles dissolved in water.

The historical geologist, then, searches for fossils that will give him more information about the earth's history. He is not often lucky enough to find a whole tree or animal. Usually, he finds bits and pieces of animals and plants that must be fitted together. The geologist must know enough about plants and animals to piece these bits together and learn what the complete specimen looked like. Even when this is done, there is still the problem of deciding how old the fossil may be. This is called "dating" the fossil. It is a very difficult and complex process. The geologist uses chemical methods to date most things. He must have a good knowledge of the earth's history so that he can fit the fossils into the right time period.

The Geological Era

When we study the history of the United States, we usually begin with the first colonies and study the Colonial Period. Then we study the early history of the United States to the Civil War. It is easier to divide the whole history into periods and study the periods one at a time. Of course, history doesn't really happen that way. History moves on at a steady pace. But it helps the student to divide history into periods marked off by major changes of some sort.

To help organize their work, the geologists, too, have divided the history of the earth into different time periods. These periods are called *geologic eras,* or geologic time periods. In a regular course in geology, many such periods are studied. They are based, very broadly, upon the kind of living things found on earth at different times. The geologist must deal with four billion years of history. He cannot be as accurate as a historian who deals with a few hundred years of time.

In our study we will consider only the five largest time divisions that geologists use in their work. Each of these periods may be subdivided into many smaller periods for more accuracy. But we do not have enough time to do that in this kind of introductory study. As you study them, notice how the time periods are based upon the type of plant and animal life on earth.

You will notice that each era has certain characteristics of its own. You will also see how plant and animal life on earth grows more complicated with each passing era. In the beginning, plants and animals were very simple. Gradually they grew more and more complicated. Finally there came the age of mammals, or warm-blooded animals, and then the age of man.

The Archeozoic Era

We know far less about the early history of the earth than we would like to. Very few solid facts are known about the earth four billion years ago. No fossils were made then, because there were no living things to make fossils. Most of our beliefs about this era are only theories. They cannot be proved. All the geologist can do is try to provide a reasonable explanation of how the earth may have developed as it is now.

The earliest period of earth history shows no signs of life. It is called the *Archeozoic era.* It lasted from the beginning of the earth until some 500 millions of years later. The earth probably began life as a body of hot gas and liquid. The Archeozoic era was the cooling off period. As the hot gases cooled, they turned into hot liquids. When the hot liquids cooled, they became solid rocks. Finally, a thin crust began to form on the surface of the earth. In the beginning the crust was thin and weak. It broke often. More hot liquid spilled over the crust, like the filling from a cherry pie in a hot oven. The weight of the liquid rock pressed the crust downward. This caused the crust to rise in other areas.

All this time the earth was slowly cooling. When it became cool enough, water began to condense in the atmosphere and fall as rain. It must have rained for years and years when this process first started. Water striking the hot crust would turn to steam and move back into the atmosphere. As it cooled, it would fall once again as rain. This helped cool the earth still more. But inside the crust it remained a hot liquid.

By the end of the Archeozoic era, the crust of the earth was formed and the temperature had dropped. The oceans were formed, and the water temperature was below the boiling point.

The crust was still very thin. It probably broke often. The dry crust was hammered by wind and water for thousands and millions of years. Solid rock was ground into particles and the particles were carried off by wind and rain. Thousands of square miles of the earth's surface were shifted by the great forces at work on the earth. The top of Mount McKinley in Alaska, for example, was then below the sea. Yet this mountain top is now twenty-thousand feet above sea level.

The Proterozoic Era

The Archeozoic era ends with the beginning of life on earth. The first life probably was found in the sea. For the next billion years, plants and animals developed in the oceans. Near the end of the billion years, some plants and animals were able to live on dry land. This billion-year period is called the *Proterozoic era.* The great changes in the crust of the earth continued throughout the Proterozoic era. Some parts of the crust emerged from the sea, while some dry regions were plunged beneath the oceans. The swirling mass of hot liquid inside the earth sometimes burst the earth's crust and flooded large areas with melted rock or lava. In this very early era many of our mineral deposits were laid down. The particles of metal tended to collect in small concentrations. When the rock cooled and hardened, the metal particles remained locked in the rocks as ore.

The Paleozoic Era

The first two geologic eras bring us within 500 million years of the present. The next era begins about 500 million years ago and lasts until about 200 million years ago. It is called the *Paleozoic era.* At the beginning of this era, much of the earth was covered by water. Plant and animal life grew steadily more complicated during this time. By the end of the era, sharks and reptiles had evolved from simpler animals. A few sea animals had come partly out of the water. They lived some of the time on land and some of the time in the oceans. These land-sea animals are called *amphibians.*

Many different types of insects, too, developed during the Paleozoic era. In the plant kingdom, large ferns, trees, and mosses were very plentiful. This era produced most of the plants that went into our deposits of coal. Coal is made of the remains of dead plants. During this Paleozoic era, great numbers of ferns and plants piled up in immense heaps when they died. The pressure on the bottom layers of plants eventually produced coal. We will learn more about coal in another unit.

The Paleozoic era also produced many changes in the crust of the earth. The Appalachian Mountains in the eastern part of the United States began to rise above the surface during this era. High sheets of ice, called glaciers, formed at the North and the South Poles. The oceans dropped lower and lower as more water was caught and held in the form of ice. Wind and water continued to carve the surface of the land that was above the seas.

The Mesozoic Era

The Paleozoic era ended about 200 million years ago. It was followed by a period called the *Mesozoie era*. This period lasted until some seventy million years ago. During the Mesozoic era, most of the animals on earth changed so they had to live either in the water or on dry land. Most of the amphibians found at the beginning of the era disappeared before the end of it. Warm-blooded animals appeared toward the end of the Mesozoic era. This was a great step forward for animals. Before this time, all animals adjusted their temperature to fit their environment. (The body temperature of birds and mammals remains approximately the same at all times.) Their organs gradually became more complex and better balanced. By the end of the era, animals had developed hard bones instead of soft gristle. This also marked a great step forward. Even today the shark does not have hard bones in its body. Bony fish appeared in large nunbers during the Mesozoic era.

On land, during this era, the first cone-bearing trees appeared on earth. The Rocky Mountains began to push above the surface of the earth. The Appalachian Mountains were now lifted high into the air, and erosion was at work carving them down to size once again.

The real masters of the earth during the Mesozoic era were the reptiles. Some had wings and others lived chiefly in the water. But reptiles dominated the earth. Probably the most fearsome of all reptiles was the *Tyrannosaurus Rex*. He was probably the most terrible monster that ever lived. With his huge teeth, powerful claws, and great strength, he could handle any other living animal in his time. For some reason we do not really understand, the age of reptiles passed. The giant reptiles died out.

The Cenozoic Era

The last of our geologic eras is called the *Cenozoic era. It* has lasted about 70 million years. This era might be called the age of the mammals. Warm-blooded animals have replaced the reptiles as kings of the earth. Reptiles, like birds, are hatched from eggs. Mammals are born alive and nursed by the mother. They are the most complex animals on earth. During the Cenozoic era, the mammals tool; control of the earth. The first elephant and the first horse appeared in this late era. Steadily the animal life kept growing more complex. The changes in the earth's surface also continued as before. The Grand Canyon began to take shape about 25 million years ago.

The Last Million Years

We have covered millions of years of earth history very briefly. But we have not yet caught sight of man. He appears on the scene as one of the mammals, perhaps one million years ago. For thousands of years man progressed very slowly. Then, in the last few thousand years, the age of man has blossomed suddenly. Today man is the dominant animal on earth. No other animal stands a chance of pushing him aside.

Another remarkable feature of the last million years has been the "Ice Ages." Four times the earth has grown cold. Ice sheets have advanced from the poles toward the Equator. At times North America was covered with solid ice as far south as New York City. After each time the climate has turned warm and the ice has melted. For the past 25,000 years the climate has been steady. Scientists do not know whether a new ice age is brewing or whether the day of ice ages is past. You will learn some of the effects of these ice ages in the chapters that follow.

6

CHAPTER II. INSIDE THE EARTH

In our last chapter we learned about the early history of the earth and how plant and animal life developed. In this chapter we will look below the crust of the earth to see what the inside is like. We will also take a look at the crust, since this is where we make our homes and earn our living. Man has never been able to penetrate very far into the earth. The deepest mines are only about two miles deep. Below this level we have not been able to move, except with oil drilling equipment. Such drills have been able to reach a four-mile depth.

Many important questions about the interior of the earth need to be answered. Beneath the crust are there, perhaps, large mineral resources that we could use? Why does the crust move and produce earthquakes? Is the interior of the earth growing warmer or colder? These and many other questions are being investigated by modern science as quickly as possible.

A Cross Section of the Earth

An observer on the moon would see the earth as a smooth, round ball, almost as smooth as a grapefruit. To us, the earth does not seem very smooth. If we compare it with a grapefruit, a dent in the grapefruit only 1/16 of an inch deep would be the same as a canyon on earth forty miles deep. From the top of our highest mountain to the bottom of the deepest valley, the distance is only thirteen miles. This is about like 1/100 of one inch on a six-inch grapefruit. The surface of the grapefruit may appear like mountains and valleys to a germ sitting in the rind. To us the grapefruit is quite smooth. The earth would look smooth too if we could stand far back and look at it.

If the earth were sliced exactly in half, it would look like the figure below. The total diameter of the slice would be about eight thousand miles. To be more exact, it is 3,960 miles from the crust to the center. Below the crust, the earth is arranged in layers like an onion. Some of the layers are easy to distinguish. Other layers are still changing as forces within the earth exert pressure on then. The thickness of the layers also varies. In fact, some geologists believe that the layers inside the earth are constantly changing.

We live on the thin outer layer, which is called the crust, of the earth. Actually, the crust is very thin when compared to the size of the entire earth. It is like the peel on a cherry. All of our minerals and other resources are obtained from this crust.

We really live on only one-fourth of the surface of the earth's crust. The rest is covered by oceans. Below the oceans the crust of the earth is a little thinner than it is on dry land. But it is made of the same materials, and it was formed in the same way. It probably contains the same kind of resources. But the ocean floor is harder to get at than dry land. So it has not been used much as a source of raw material. It may yet become an important supply region for man.

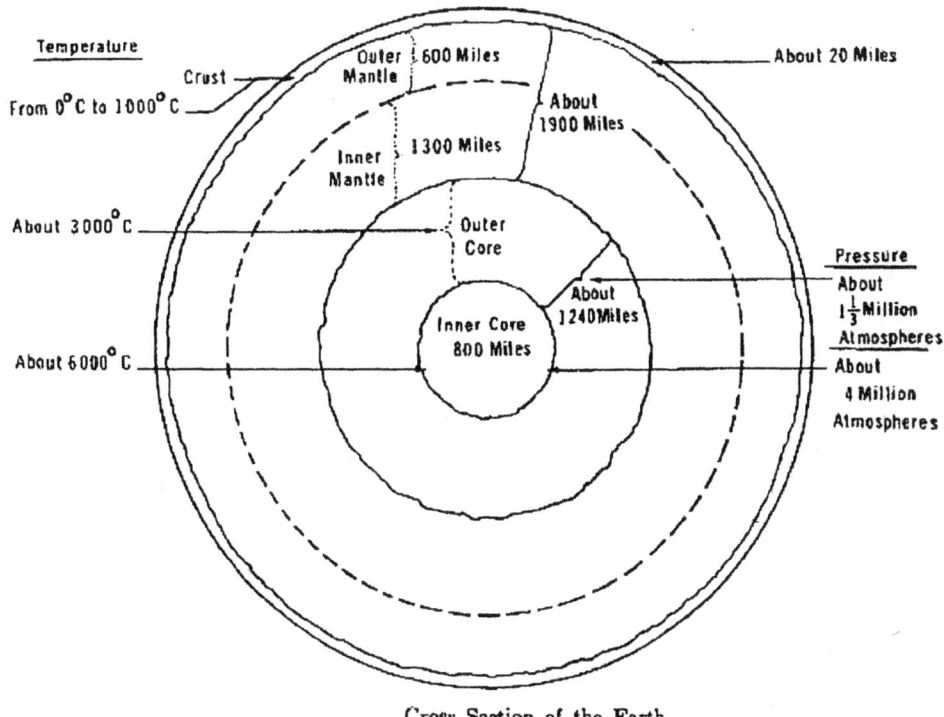

Cross Section of the Earth.

The Mantle

Below the thin crust of the earth there lies a very thick layer of rock called the *mantle*. This mantle is usually divided into two parts - the *outer mantle*, about six hundred miles thick, and the *inner mantle*, about thirteen hundred miles thick. Lying below the outer mantle, the inner one makes up most of the volume of the earth. The rock in the outer mantle is solid, but it is lighter, or less dense, than the rock in the inner mantle. The great pressure on the inner mantle forces the rock molecules together and increases the density. The outer mantle is probably made of material like the crust of the earth. The inner mantle may contain heavier elements, since it weighs more than the rock in the outer mantle.

The Core

If we compare the earth to a cherry, the thin skin of the cherry is like the earth's crust. The part of the cherry we eat is like the inner and outer mantles put together. The pit of the cherry is like the core of the earth. It is heavier and more solid than the outer parts of the earth. For a scientist, the core of the earth is a liquid. But it is not a liquid like water or oil. A scientist calls all matter a liquid if it behaves in a certain way. For example, certain kinds of earthquake shock waves that are transmitted by solids are not transmitted by liquids. The core of the earth will not transmit these waves. Therefore, the earth's core is called a liquid. But it must be a very thick, heavy liquid, under great pressure. For the material in the core of the earth weighs about five times as much as the material in the outer crust. That is, the core of the earth is very dense and heavy.

Geologists divide the core of the earth into two parts: an inner core and an outer core. The temperature in the inner core is probably about the same as the temperature on the surface of the sun, that is 6,000°C. The pressure is very high because of the weight of the upper layers of the earth. The core probably contains nickel and iron, which are very heavy. The scientists who study the core believe it may contain other material even more dense than nickel. That is why core material is five times as dense as material from the crust.

The Geologist at Work

If we cannot look inside the earth, how does the scientist learn all of these facts about the interior? The geologist must learn about the inside of the earth in the same way a doctor studies a broken arm without cutting the arm open. The doctor uses a small machine to produce x-rays. The geologist uses a natural machine of great power. He uses the waves generated by earthquakes. When an earthquake occurs, shock waves are sent out through the earth. These waves are timed and recorded by machines called *seismographs*. The record does not look like an x-ray picture. But a trained geologist can "read" the recording just as a trained doctor "reads" an x-ray. Most of our information about the interior of the earth is obtained by this method. It is called the science of *seismology*.

When some part of the earth's crust breaks apart, a great disturbance may be caused, which we call an earthquake. Earthquakes carry an immense amount of energy. If you break a stick in your hands, you can feel the shock run through your body. An earthquake produces the same effect. When great pressure causes the crust to snap, shock waves travel through the earth from the break. These waves can create great damage if they tear the surface open. A strong shock wave can tear an entire city apart in a few minutes. A large earthquake generates more power than millions of hydrogen bombs.

The geologist studies these shock waves with his seismograph. He measures the time it takes for the waves to travel through the earth. You can picture the earthquake as a transmitter. The seismograph acts as a radio receiver which receives a special type of message. By making many readings of earthquakes and comparing the results, the geologist can make a map of the interior of the earth.

The figure below shows you how seismology works. An earthquake has taken place at point A. The crust has snapped, and powerful shock waves are moving away from A through the earth. Suppose that points B, C, and D are seismographs. Each seismograph will receive a shock wave at a different time. By comparing the travel time of the waves, geologists learn about the interior. By careful checking and comparing, geologists have prepared the drawing of the earth which you see in the figure below.

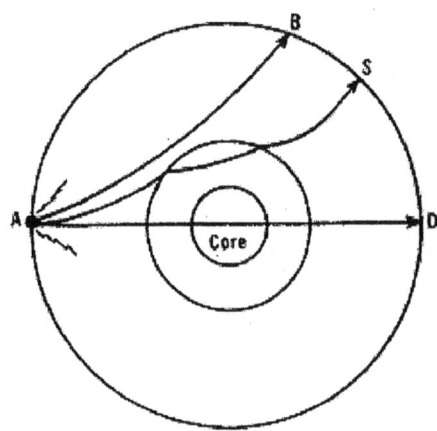

More About the Crust

Where the crust of the earth is smooth and flat, the people may have excellent farm land. Where the crust is wrinkled and torn, the land may be mountainous and of no use for farming. Where there are large mineral deposits and a supply of fuel, like coal, in the crust, the people who live there may develop a good supply of industries. Where the crust is poor in resources, the people may not be able to build large factories and machines. You can see that the condition of the crust is a matter of great importance to all of us.

There are ninety-two different natural elements found on earth, each made of a different kind of atom. All of these elements appear in the crust. But most of the crust is made of just two elements -silicon and oxygen, which are usually found tied with other elements in some compound. The most common elements are shown in the following table.

You can see that three-fourths of all the material in the crust is made of combinations of oxygen or silicon. Sand, for example, is made of silicon and oxygen; so you can see how plentiful these elements are in the crust.

The crust is made almost entirely of rock. Rocks vary in density. Some are light; others are thick and heavy. We will study the different types of rock in the next chapter. The temperature of the crust varies from freezing in some points at the top to about 1,000°C at the bottom of the crust. The pressure increases as we go down into the earth. In addition, radioactivity releases heat into the crust. In fact, some scientists believe that the earth may be growing warmer because of the amount of radioactivity in the crust.

Element	Approximate Percent of Crust	Element	Approximate Percent of Crust
Oxygen	47	Sodium	3
Silicon	28	Potassium	3
Aluminum	8	Magnesium	2
Iron	5	Others	1
Calcium	4		

Soil

A farmer with a farm made of solid rock could not grow food. Plants must have not only sunlight to grow; they must also have a supply of water, minerals, and carbon dioxide. The water and minerals cone from the earth. All living plants except those that live in the oceans are found growing in a very thin layer of rock particles and dead plant and animal material on top of the solid rock. This mixture is what we call *soil.* The layer of soil on the earth is hundreds of feet thick in some places. In other areas, there is no soil at all. The bare solid rock is exposed to the air and sun. In these bare regions few plants will grow.

Soil is produced by the action of wind and water in the process called *weathering.* Large chunks of rock are broken down into tiny rock particles. These tiny particles are mixed with bits of dead animal and vegetable matter to form soil. We will study the weathering process in another chapter. It is sometimes hard to believe that all of the loose soil on earth was once solid rock and plant life. Of course, it takes thousands or millions of years to produce these fine soil particles. But nature is in no hurry.

Conposition of Soil

Soil also contains tiny living organisms. They are called *micro-organisms* because they can be seen only with a microscope. These tiny living creatures are essential for plant life. Some micro-organisms have the ability to take nitrogen from the air and prepare it for use by the plants. A plant must have nitrogen to grow, but it cannot use nitrogen from the air. It obtains nitrogen through the work of these tiny bacteria, or micro-organisms. The bacteria take nitrogen from the air and make it into nitrates. When the nitrates dissolve in water, they can be used by plants. This is one more example of the remarkable way that the natural world is balanced.

The composition of soil is changing constantly. Plants take minerals from the soil to build their bodies. These soil minerals must be replaced before more plants will grow. If the plant dies and is buried on the same spot where it grew, some material is actually replaced in the soil. But if we take the plant away and eat it, we must do something to add the minerals which the plant used up to build its body.

Farriers return minerals to the soil by using *fertilizers.* Some fertilizers are waste materials from animals. Others are prepared commercially by chemical companies. In some cases, the farmers grow special crops and plow them back into the earth to restore the minerals to the soil and keep it fertile. Different crops use different minerals . The farmer must learn how to repair his soil scientifically. That is what is meant by *scientific farming.* The U.S. Department of Agriculture helps farmers find out exactly what a certain crop takes from the soil and what he must do to return that substance to the soil.

Erosion

Finally, the soil can be carried away by wind or water. This is called *erosion.* It is one of the great problems farmers must face. Ground that is covered with grass and trees will not blow away easily. But when the ground is plowed for farming, the soil is loosened and its protective coat is stripped away. It can then be blown away in dust storms or washed away by water. There are ways to prevent this loss of soil too. But it requires a careful conservation program. Otherwise, the topsoil needed to grow food can be lost. It is true that eventually nature will produce more soil by weathering the solid rock and breaking it into particles. But this takes a very long tine.

CHAPTER III. ROCKS AND MINERALS

We learned in the last chapter that when the crust of the earth hardened, it formed solid rock. For millions and millions of years the weather has been attacking this solid rock and breaking it down into smaller particles. Wind and rain and ice have all helped break rock up into the smaller bits by the process called *weathering.* The small rock particles, mixed with dead animal and vegetable material, called *soil,* form a thin layer. This layer covers parts of the earth and supplies the farmland that provides our food supply. When we dig down through the layer of soil, we find a layer of solid bedrock underneath. This bedrock may be very close to the surface, or it may be buried beneath many feet of loose soil. But it will always be found if we dig deep enough into the earth.

Soils

The layer of soil on top of the earth's crust can be divided into two parts. At the very top is a thin layer of fine particles, called *topsail.* This is the soil needed to grow plants. Below the topsoil is a layer of material called *subsoil.* Some subsoils are made of thick, heavy clay. Others are thin and loose and mixed with small stones or gravel. Whatever the material in the subsoil, it too is made from solid rock by weathering.

Some of the best farming land in the world was produced by a thick deposit of topsoil, carried along by wind or water. In northern China and in Argentina the wind has piled up very deep deposits of fine, rich soil. These dust deposits are called *loess.* Some of the loess deposits in China are more than a thousand feet thick. Thinner deposits of loess are found in Argentina and along the Mississippi River in the United States. Of course, the area where the wind removed the soil was stripped to make these deep, rich soil deposits.

Other rich farm areas have been produced by soil carried along by running water. The Nile River, the Mississippi River, and the Ganges River in India have all produced deep banks of rich soil at the river mouth. This type of soil deposit is called a *delta.* A delta is made of rich fine soil, carried to the mouth of the river by the current. It is excellent soil for farming.

Rocks

The earth's crust was once liquid rock. When the hot liquids on the earth cooled, a solid layer of rock was formed on the top. All our soil has been produced from this original rock surface by weathering. Since the original crust was formed, many new layers of rock have been formed. Geologists divide all rocks into three main types. Each type was made in a different way. Each rock has different characteristics.

Igneous Rock

When melted rock hardens to form a solid mass, it is called *igneous rook.* All of the original crust of the earth was made of igneous rock. This original crust has since been buried under thick layers of rock particles and vegetation.

Igneous rock is hard and durable. Two common types of igneous rock are *granite* and *basalt.* Both contain several different minerals. In granite we usually find some quartz, mica, and a mineral called feldspar. The quartz in granite is hard and glassy. The other minerals may be pink, gray, or black in color. Granite is a very tough stone which is used for heavy buildings. Basalt is a hard, dark-colored rock, which is not quite as strong as granite. After a volcano erupts, basalt is usually formed when the lava hardens. Because of its strength and availability, basalt is used for road construction and other jobs that require wearing ability and hardness.

Sedimentary Rock

When wind and water carry great piles of stone particles and store them in one place, a deep layer of material builds up. This layer is heavy, and it creates a strong pressure on the bottom of the pile. This pressure can force the particles of stone back together and fuse them into solid rock. Rocks that are formed by pressure of this sort are called *sedimentary* rocks. Sedimentary rock usually forms in layers. It looks like plywood. It is not nearly so strong as igneous rock, since sedimentary rocks are often formed from weaker minerals and the particles are not bound as strongly as those of igneous rocks, which were welded together by heat.

Three common sedimentary rocks are *limestone, shale,* and *sandstone.* Most *limestone* is formed from the bodies of tiny sea animals. Although it is mined on dry land, the deposits of limestone were originally nade beneath the oceans. This stone is whitish in color. It is used in steelmaking because it helps remove impurities from the iron.

Sandstone is made of tiny grains of sand that have been pressed together into a solid block. The sand is sometimes held together by a nixture of iron and oxygen, which we call rust. The chemist calls the mixture *iron oxide.* It is usually red, and it colors the sandstone. Because the color is attractive, sandstone is often used for building material.

Shale is a very soft rock formed in thin, weak layers. The layers are filled with airspace. Oil is found stored in the airspaces in a special type of shale.

Most of the fossils studied by geologists appear in sedimentary rocks, not in igneous rock. No fossil could survive the heat that goes into forming of igneous rock. But sedimentary rock takes a good impression when a plant or animal is trapped in it.

Metamorphic Rock

If any type of rock is heated to high enough temperatures, it will melt. Very great pressure will also cause changes in the structure of rock. Any rock that changes its form because of heat or pressure is called *metamorphic* rock. Metamorphic means *changed.* Rocks which have changed from one type to another fall into this group. Such changes may be brought about in several ways. Hot melted rock can flow up to the surface and melt the rock it touches. An earthquake can shift the rock inside the earth and allow hot liquid rock to move into a new area. The weight of a mountain range will some-tines change the rock beneath it to produce metamorphic rock.

You have probably seen a slate blackboard in a schoolroom. The color may be black or green or even gray. Usually it is black. This is a metamorphic rock. Slate was once shale rock, but it has been heated and compressed to form slate.

Marble is another common metamorphic rock. White marble is made from pure limestone. But most marble is streaked with color. This color depends upon the minerals in the original rock. Marble can easily be polished to a fine finish. It is used for decorating public buildings and for making tombstones.

Coal, Graphite, and Diamonds

Coal is often grouped as a type of metamorphic rock. There are several different types of coal. Each type is known by its hardness. Since all coal is made by the same process, all types of coal contain the same material. Hard coal, which is very important to us, is coal that has been pressed very hard.

Coal is made from dead plant and animal matter that builds up in great heaps. As the layers of material get deeper, the pressure on the bottom increases. This squeezes out some of the water. The temperature also increases, and the mixture at the bottom gradually hardens. The first stage of the process produces a soft, crumbly material called *peat*. Peat is a mixture of carbon and water and sone other minerals. It will burn, but it is very smoky and does not make good fuel.

As the peat is compressed and heated still more, it grows harder. More water is forced out. This leaves a higher percentage of carbon. By this process the next stage in coalmaking takes place. A poor grade of coal is formed, called *lignite*. It is also called *brown coal*. Brown coal also will burn, but it too makes a great deal of smoke and not much heat.

When brown coal is further compressed and heated, it is changed into *soft coal,* or *bituminous coal.* Soft coal is the most common fuel on earth. In fact, there is probably more of it in the world than of any other single material. Soft coal is a key material in many processes. When it is roasted, it forms *coke,* which is used to produce steel. When soft coal is burned, the gases can be used for many types of chemicals. Most of the electricity used in the United States is manufactured by burning soft coal, which powers electric generators. In other words, soft coal is a very important mineral. It produces electric power; and it forms the basic substance used to make dyes, plastics, and many other chemical materials.

But when coal has been compressed still more, so that nearly all the water has been driven out, we have *hard coal,* or *anthracite coal.* Hard coal is an ideal fuel for heating the house. It burns without smoke and leaves little ash. Most of the water has been removed, so that this coal is almost pure carbon. The supply of anthracite coal, however, is not large. Soft coal is far more common.

If hard coal is compressed until the last bit of water is removed, all that remains is pure carbon. A diamond is a special type of pure carbon. So is the material called *graphite*. Graphite is used for the "lead" in pencils and also as a dry lubricant in machinery.

Ores

An ore is a rock that contains minerals. In order to be an ore, a rock must contain enough minerals to be mined at a profit. Many rocks contain some minerals. But they are not ores because the minerals are not worth mining. The type of mineral in an ore may be metal or nonmetal.

The supply of ore in the world is not spread evenly in the earth's crust. Some countries, like the United States and Russia, have rich supplies of ore. Other areas have little or no ore in their part of the crust. Much of Africa and Asia seem to have little ore that can be used to build modern industry. Sometimes we find very valuable ores in small pockets. In Canada, for example, a few mines furnish a large part of the world's supply of nickel. This metal is used to harden steel. Diamonds are found chiefly in South Africa. Even coal is not found in every part of the earth. Since modern industry depends upon fuel and minerals, countries which have none cannot hope to become industrial powers without help from the outside.

<u>Oil, or Petroleum</u>

One of the most valuable minerals in our day is petroleum, or oil. Petroleum produces fuel for automobiles, diesel engines, and jet aircraft. It is used to make dyes and plastics. In fact, innumerable products are made from petroleum. We will study some of these products more closely in another chapter.

Oil is found in pools under the surface of the earth. We do not know what oil is made from; it probably begins as dead plant and animal matter, which seems to form in the sea, for salt water is usually found with the oil pools. There is often a supply of natural gas with the oil. When a well is tapped, the pressure of the gas can cause oil to rise through the pipes and to create a "gusher." The oil pools are usually found in layers of sandstone. This rock has many small air pockets that can contain the oil. The oil pool is often covered by a hard dome of solid rock. This holds the oil pool below the surface. A typical oil dome is shown in the figure below. The oil is found in the layer of porous rock. The hard dome above the oil pool holds in the natural gas and the oil.

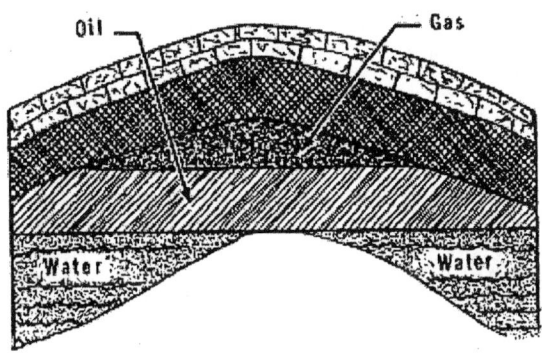

Men tap the oil dome by drilling a hole down through the rock cover. If there is enough gas pressure, the oil will bubble from the well. But most oil wells must be pumped. If carefully drilled, an oil dome can be made to produce both petroleum and natural gas. Look at the figure above. A pipe inserted at the point in the dome marked A would bring out natural gas. A pipe at point B would produce petro-leum. Both of these products are valuable. Unless the natural gas is tapped carefully, it will escape and be lost.

When petroleum comes from a well, it is a black or brown sticky liquid. Before it can be used, it must be processed. This is called *refining*. The oil coming from a well actually contains dozens of different materials. Most of them can be used and are valuable. In an oil refinery these parts of petroleum are separated. Then the different products produced from petroleum can be manufactured and prepared for marketing.

Geologists use the same method to search for oil that they use to study the interior of the earth. They use a seismograph, and they study the picture they get when a shock wave passes through the crust. But an oil geologist need not wait for an earthquake. He does not need such a large shock. He can set off a charge of blasting powder. This is the method usually employed. The shock from the powder is recorded by the seismograph. A skilled geologist can tell from the seismograph whether it is possible that oil may lie beneath the surface. He cannot be certain, and drilling oil wells is always an expensive gamble. But oil is a valuable product, and oil companies can afford to spend large amounts of money to locate new supplies of it.

CHAPTER IV. CHANGING THE FACE OF THE EARTH

For years the face of the earth has been changing steadily. Once the crust had formed on the earth, wind and water acted to wear it down into tiny particles. New parts of the crust have been shoved high into the air to form mountains. Then these mountains have been worn away again by wind and water. This process has been going on for millions and millions of years.

The crust of the earth, that began as solid rock, is today covered with plant life and with the particles of rock mixed with dead plant and animal matter that we call soil. Several factors go into this weathering, or breaking down of solid rock into tiny particles. The chief ones are wind, water, and sudden temperature changes. In time even the mightiest rock can be worn away by these forces.

Erosion

Weathering produces tiny particles of rock. When the solid rock is broken into smaller pieces, which are moved away from where they were forned, we call the process *erosion*. The chief causes of erosion are the same wind, water, and temperature changes that cause weathering. In fact, many people think of weathering as part of the whole process of erosion. In the end, erosion brings most of the tiny rock particles to the bottom of the sea. When the weight of them is heavy enough to cause the crust to sink, another part of the crust is thrust into the air. Then erosion begins all over again. Thus, by weathering and erosion a thick blanket of rock particles, or soil, has been built up on the face of the earth. As you already know, some of these particles become welded into solid sedimentary rock by the pressure of the particles on top of the heap.

Movements of the Earth's Crust

The ground under our feet always seems quite solid and firm. But the earth's crust is also flexible. When it is pressed down in one area, it will rise up somewhere else. When wind and water pile sediment on it until it becomes heavy, or when a large icecap forms on it, the crust sinks down to a lower level under the added weight. To compensate, or make up for this sinking, another part of the crust rises higher. This has happened over and over again. Parts of the earth that are dry today were once at the bottom of the sea.

The northern part of North America was once covered by a large, heavy glacier. This mass of ice weighed down the crust until it sank. When the glacier melted, the Great Lakes and Hudson Bay were formed. Now that the ice is gone, this area is slowly rising. Some day it nay rise high enough to cause the water to leave Hudson Bay and flow back into the ocean.

When the solid parts of the earth's crust shift, the movement is called *diastrophism*. These shifts happen quite often. Once in a while a change takes place on a very large scale. Hundreds of miles of crust are pressed into the air to form mountain ranges. Parts of a whole continent may sink beneath the sea. Of course, these changes take place very slowly. The earth does not usually move quickly. We are not likely to wake up and find a new mountain outside our window, though the earth can produce a small volcanic peak in a few weeks.

Vulcanism

When the great masses of hot melted rock move or cause changes in the earth's crust, the process is called *vulcanism.* The word has the same base as *volcanoes,* for volcanoes represent a particular kind of vulcanism. Great floods of molten rock pour across the hard crust of the earth. Some of these floods may cover thousands of square miles. Giant mountain peaks can be built by this process. The Hawaiian Islands are made almost entirely of volcanic rock thrust up from inside the earth. The flow of hot lava, or melted rock, can occur under the oceans or on dry land. Vulcanism is still going on today, for the earth is still hot inside. It can generate great pressures that can cause its crust to move.

Water Erosion

Even today a great flood can bring modern cities to a complete stop. This gives an indication of the power of running water. Even the smallest stream, if it is given time, can chew a great hole in the earth. Water is the most effective earthmover on the surface of the earth. Volcanic activity may look more spectacular and powerful. But in the long run, water does more to change the face of the earth than any other force. Every day billions of tons of water rise from the oceans and drop on the land. Each year enough water falls on earth to cover the whole surface with thirty inches of water. As it runs over dry land, it picks up particles of rock and soil and carries them along. If you ever watch a fast creek running in the spring of the year, you are likely to find the water brightly colored with earth. Given time, a trickle of water will wear away the strongest rocks. In a few thousand years, water can carve a Grand Canyon across the face of the earth.

Water that is carrying particles of rock is an even more effective eroding agent than pure water. The rock particles act like sandpaper, scraping away at the sides of the creek or river. Usually this is a slow process. But water, too, can act quickly. A sudden cloudburst can bring a torrent down a hillside, sweeping away the farmer's fields and his crops. That is why farmers are particularly concerned with water erosion. If the water carries away their topsoil, plants cannot grow.

The amount of erosion caused by running water depends upon two factors. First, since water running over solid rock will not carry away as much of the surface as water running over loose soil, *the type of surface is one factor that determines erosion.* Second, since slow moving water erodes much less soil than a fast moving stream, *the rate of travel is another and a major factor in water erosion.* In a slow stream the silt falls to the bottom and is not carried very far. When the speed of flow is doubled, the ability of the water to carry soil is increased many times. The soil particles give the water more cutting power as they strike against the banks.

Chemical Action of Water

If you place some salt in a glass of water, the water will dissolve the salt. Water has the ability to dissolve many different minerals. When water reaches the minerals in rock, it often dissolves them. This weakens the rock and makes it easier to break apart. Water also expands about 10 percent in volume when it freezes. In cold climates this expansion power of water can split very large rocks. Liquid water can enter a crack in a rock and freeze there. The expansion of the water when it forms ice acts like a wedge. Many blocks of stone are broken off the earth's crust by this process. When the solid block is removed, the face of the crust is again exposed to the erosion of wind and water.

Wind Erosion

During the 1930's, the central part of the United States was often called the Dust Bowl. There had been little rain, and the ground became a dry, thin powder. This powder was picked up by the wind and carried for hundreds of miles across the country. Millions of acres of good farmland were nearly ruined by the erosion caused by the wind. Water causes more erosion than wind; but in dry climates, where there is little water, the wind can also cut away the earth's crust.

When the wind blows hard, it picks up particles of rock and soil and carries them along. These particles give the wind a cutting edge. In fact, they make it act like a regular sandblast. The tiny particles strike against the earth and wear through solid stone very quickly. This sandblasting effect can cause odd-looking rock formations. The wind cannot raise the rock particles high in the air, so most of the cutting effect is felt close to the ground. This carves the part of the stone near the ground faster than the part high in the air.

Other Types of Erosion

When a piece of solid rock is heated and then cooled very quickly, the outer parts of the rock contract more rapidly than the inside. This places a terrific strain on the rock and can cause it to split apart. In the deserts, where the temperature falls very quickly after sundown, this type of action takes place often. Travelers in the desert may hear a loud snap like a cannon shot when a huge rock splits apart.

Plants and animals also help break down the solid crust of the earth. Plant roots work into the cracks and split the rock apart as they grow. Sometimes a large tree will grow right through the center of a solid piece of rock, splitting it apart. Waste matter from the bodies of plants and animals also produces chemicals that affect the minerals in rock. When an animal, however small, digs a hole beneath a large rock, wind and water are enabled to reach a larger surface area of the rock. This, too, increases the speed of erosion slightly. Each of these effects seems very small. But nature works steadily and slowly. Any little additional help will make some difference in the long run.

The climate can affect the speed of weathering and erosion. In a hot, wet climate erosion tends to work faster than in a cool, dry climate. In a climate that includes freezing temperatures, expanding ice helps speed the process. Some of the buildings in Egypt lasted for thousands of years in the dry climate there. When they were taken to North America or England, the dampness speedily weathered the face of the rock. In general, the amount of moisture in the air seems to be the most important single factor in weathering.

River Valleys

Most of the great valleys on earth, like the Grand Canyon, have been dug by rivers. A river needs thousands of years to dig a Grand Canyon. It can produce a smaller valley in a much shorter time. All that is needed is a good supply of water and the force of gravity. All water returns to the oceans eventually, digging a valley in the earth as it returns. Scientists have found that rivers follow a regular pattern of growth.

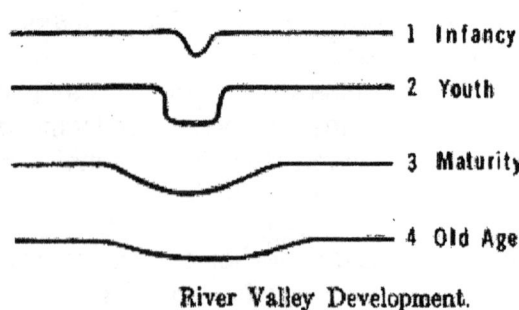

River Valley Development.

One heavy rainfall can begin a great river valley. Suppose a heavy rain digs a small trench in the earth. If water continues to flow through it, this little trench can become a great river valley. As the river changes, it passes through four separate stages or periods. The figure above shows a cross-section of the river in each of these stages.

The first step cuts a sharp gulley in the earth. The sides of the gulley are V-shaped, and it is cut deep into the ground. Soon a small river is formed. As the river grows, the gulley becomes deeper but not much wider. The V-shape broadens at the bottom, as the walls of the river are cut more deeply. The weight of the water on the river bottom helps speed the cutting process. When the bottom is cut down to full depth, the river valley has reached its young stage. The valley continues to broaden and smooth out. The curves of the river become more gradual. The edges of the valley become rounded off by the wind and water. In time the river moves more and more slowly. It carries a large amount of solid and rock particles. The river adds more twists and turns as it moves along. The valley becomes very broad and smooth - like a rolling dip in the landscape. The river is then in its *old age.*

The Mississippi River is in its old age at the present time. It flows in broad gentle curves, carrying a heavy load of silt. A great delta has been built up at the mouth of the Mississippi. This river carries about half a billion tons of silt into the ocean each year. The Mississippi is really an "Old Man River," though it can still break loose and cause enormous amounts of damage during a flood.

Preventing Erosion

Weathering, the breaking of solid rock into particles, is a good thing for human beings. It increases the supply of soil. But erosion, which moves these particles toward the sea, is a catastrophe. The soil is often lost for all time at the bottom of the sea. Nature has her own way of controlling this damage. A layer of strong grass and trees will reduce erosion to a minimum. But once the trees are cut and the grass is plowed, wind and water can act directly against the soft soil. Wind erosion in the 1930's carried Kansas topsoil onto the decks of ships in the middle of the Atlantic Ocean. Much of this erosion was due to careless farming.

Today farmers are aware of the need for erosion control. The U.S. Department of Agriculture and the state governments help reduce the loss of soil due to erosion. Large stands of trees have been planted to break the force of wind. Farmers have learned how to plant their crops in ways that reduce erosion. Dams have been built to control flooding. But we still lose millions of tons of topsoil every year. We must learn to take care of the land if we are going to provide for the future. It is one of our most valuable possessions.

CHAPTER V. GLACIERS

The land at the South Pole is covered by a layer of solid ice thousands of feet thick. This sheet of ice moves across the continent of Antarctica toward the sea. A moving "river" of ice is called a *glacier*. A glacier that covers a large region like Antarctica is called an *icecap*. Glaciers are found in cold climates like the North Pole and the South Pole, or high in the mountains where snow accumulates faster than it can melt.

A glacier is a moving body of very heavy solid ice. It can cause great changes in the crust of the earth. As the glacier passes over the land, its force can grind large rocks to powder and strip away all loose material. Glaciers also affect the climate of the earth and the water level in the oceans. If large glaciers should form on earth, cities like New York might find themselves hundreds of miles from the ocean because of the water taken from the ocean to form the glaciers. Or if the glaciers now on earth should melt, New York would be submerged beneath more than one hundred feet of water. Glaciers are still an important force on earth, though it appears that our glaciers are slowly melting at the present time.

Location of Glaciers

About 10 percent of the land area of the earth is covered by glaciers. One whole continent - Antarctica - is covered by a single large icecap. This Antarctic glacier alone is larger than the entire United States. It is several thousand feet thick in spots, and it contains about 85 percent of the world's ice. Another 10 percent of the glacial ice in the world is concentrated in the icecap in Greenland. The remainder is divided among the hundreds of small glaciers found in the mountains around the world. Glaciers may be a few hundred feet thick or thousands of feet thick. They may be only a few miles long or very huge like the glacier in Antarctica.

Why Glaciers Form

Glaciers form because the climate is cold enough to produce solid ice. No one knows why the climate should change enough to cause glaciers to form. We do not know why the climate changes again and causes glaciers to melt and grow smaller. But we do know that this has happened several times in the past million years. Four times the glaciers in the world have grown much larger. As much as 30 percent of the earth has been covered by glaciers at one time. That is about three times as much coverage as we have at the present time.

During the ice ages, the climate must have turned cold. The oceans were two hundred to three hundred feet lower than they are today. Great sheets of ice covered much of northern Europe and North America and northern Asia. The entire earth must have been fairly cool. Yet the earth grew warmer once again, and the glaciers began to melt.

Today the glaciers are only 1/3 as large as they were at their peak period. We do not know why this change occurred. Nor do we know if the climate may suddenly turn cold once more and the glaciers again begin to grow. We seem to be living in a period when the earth is growing warmer. But we cannot be certain that this is true.

How Glaciers Form

All glaciers begin life as falling snow. If the climate is cold, not all of the snow that falls will melt in the year. In time a thick layer of snow can pile up on the earth's crust. That is why glaciers are found near the poles or high in the mountains. Snow must remain on the ground throughout the year before a glacier can form.

When the pile of snow is thick enough, the pressure on the bottom causes the snow to change into small lumps called *buckshot ice.* The next step in the process produces a layer of solid ice on the bottom of the snow pile. The process is like the formation of sedimentary rocks. Each year the ice grows thicker and heavier.

When the weight of the ice layer reaches a certain point, the force of gravity is stronger than the friction between the ice and the ground. The ice sheet then begins to move. A glacier has been born. The energy that moves the glacier is provided by gravity acting on the weight of the ice sheet. Each year more snow falls on top of it, increasing the weight of the glacier and providing the energy for further movement. We say that the new snow "feeds" the glacier. A glacier will always move from high ground to low ground. It cannot move upward. But it can cross small hills to get to a lower area on the other side. A light glacier needs a sharp slope. But a large continental glacier can move along a very slight slope once it grows heavy enough. The glacier that once covered northern North America moved steadily across the countryside. It filled in valleys and shaved off large hills as it passed.

When a glacier reaches the sea, it shoves forward into the water. Great chunks break off the solid sheet of the glacier and float out into the ocean. We call them *icebergs.*

Why Glaciers Move

The force of gravity is centered in the core of the earth. Every object on earth will move as close to the center of the earth as possible. That is why objects fall to the ground. That is why a car will roll down a hill. The glaciers moves for the same reason. It is pulled by the gravity of the earth toward the lowest possible level. So all glaciers move toward the sea. Other forces also help move a glacier over the earth. Part of the glacier may melt and then freeze again. The expansion of water when it freezes can shove the glacier along. When it crosses a hill, it bulges and cracks on top. The cracks can fill with snow and increase the forward pressure. All of these factors combine to keep the glacier moving.

Most glaciers move very slowly. A few inches of motion each day is a good average. A few have been known to move about fifty feet in one day, but that is rare. As the glacier reaches warmer temperatures, it melts at the forward edge. If the glacier melts as rapidly as it is pushed forward from behind, it will appear to stand still. Actually, it keeps moving forward, but it loses more distance than it gains. The rate of melting changes from year to year, depending upon the climate.

Icebergs

When the front edge of a glacier reaches the ocean, it is forced out into the water by the pressure behind it. When the weight of the edge is more than the glacier can support, the chunk in the ocean breaks off. It then floats off as an iceberg. Some icebergs are very large. In Antarctica, icebergs have been seen which were several miles across and thousands of feet thick.

Fortunately, icebergs from Antarctica do not move into the world's shipping lanes. But icebergs from the Arctic Ocean are a real menace to shipping. When the oceanliner Titanic struck an iceberg in 1912, more than fifteen hundred persons were lost. This does not happen often today, but a close watch must be kept on the shipping lanes. Most of the weight of an iceberg lies below the surface. An innocent looking little iceberg has about nine times as much mass below water as it shows on the surface. We can now use sonar and other electronic equipment to locate large icebergs, even in a fog. They are less dangerous than they were before this equipment was available.

Glacial Erosion

The continent of North America shows the effect of glacial erosion better than any other area. During the ice ages the glaciers that covered the northern part of the continent made great changes in the land. The weight of the ice caused the crust to sink. But the crust has been rising steadily since the glacier melted. It will be a long time before it recovers completely.

If you run a rough file over soft wood, the surface of the wood becomes splintered and torn. A glacier has this same effect on the earth. As the glacier moves along, it picks up rocks and soil particles and holds them fast. This makes a giant rasp on the bottom of the glacier. The pressure on the bottom reaches many tons for each square foot. As the glacier slides along, it rasps off the surface of the earth right down to the bedrock. Even solid rock can be cut and torn by the weight of a moving glacier. The loose rock, stones, and soil are torn off the surface and carried away. Hills are swept clean, and valleys are filled with rock and soil. Huge boulders are carried hundreds of miles, then dropped when the glacier melts. Some of the boulders that now lie in the Ohio River Valley were carried south from Canada by the glaciers.

Once the loose soil is cleared away, the glacier goes to work on the solid rock below. It tears great blocks of stone loose and grinds large rocks to powder by its weight. After a glacier passes over the land, it looks as though a land-hungry army has been marching through. The terrain is left smooth and rounded. Tops of hills are cut off, and valleys are filled in. The topsoil has just about disappeared, carried away by the glacier. Bedrock lies exposed on the surface. Even this solid rock is scratched and torn. Areas that have been visited by a glacier may be useless for farming for thousands of years. Large parts of Canada, for example, have almost no topsoil left. It was carried away by the glaciers centuries ago.

Glacial Moraine

When a glacier stops moving, it is like a child that has stopped playing with its toys. It drops everything just where it happens to be when the movement ceases. So all glaciers leave their calling cards behind. A long line of loose rocks, boulders, and other material carried by the glacier marks the point where the movement stopped. This line of debris is called a *glacial moraine.* Glaciers cannot put anything back where they found it. They move only in one direction.

A glacier can be very generous to some parts of the world. But it is generous at the expense of some other areas. The rich farmland in the north-central United States, for example, was deposited by glacial action. The Ohio River Valley and other parts of the Midwest were made rich by such deposits. So the glacier "robs Peter to pay Paul." Millions of tons of topsoil in the United States were taken from the land in Canada. In a way, the Midwestern states are rich because large areas in Canada are very poor. In the same way, the delta at the mouth of the Mississippi River is rich because the river has stolen topsoil from large areas in central United States.

Mountain Glaciers

Glaciers that form on mountain tops are usually much smaller than the large continental glaciers. But they are formed in the same way and they move in the same way. The loose soil on the mountain is stripped away, leaving sharp clear peaks of solid rock. The Alps in Europe are covered with sharp peaks formed by glacial action. Once the glacier has done its work, only solid rock remains on the mountain. In time the erosion effect of wind and water will finish the job that the glacier started.

Glaciers also create some beautiful mountain lakes. The grinding effect of the glacier can carve out a hollow spot in the mountains. The melting glacier will fill the hollow with water. Many of these mountain lakes are famous beauty spots.

Glaciers and Erosion

You can see that the erosion effect of glaciers is tremendous. Of course, they do not affect the whole world equally. But in the areas they visit, glaciers are the most powerful forces of erosion known. Fortunately, the parts of the earth which have large populations are not troubled with glaciers at the present time. And since glaciers move very slowly, the possibility of glacial damage in the near future is small. But many of the conditions we now have are the result of glacial action. And a very large part of the world has been changed by the force of glaciers moving over the surface. If the earth should grow cold once again and if the glaciers should again begin to move across the earth, more great changes would take place.

CHAPTER VI. PRESSURE INSIDE THE EARTH

If we stretch a rubberband, it will snap back into shape again. That is, the rubberband is *elastic*. It can change its shape temporarily and then return to its original shape. But if we stretch the rubberband too far, it will not return to the original shape. The size of the rubberband can be changed permanently. When a permanent change can be made in the size or shape of material, we say it is *plastic*. Like the rubberband, the crust of the earth that we live on is both elastic and plastic. The shape of the crust can be changed temporarily, and it can be changed permanently.

Because we can see only a small part of the earth's crust at one time, it looks quite solid. But a view of the whole earth shows that the crust is changing shape all the time. Some of the changes are only temporary; others are permanent. Both types of change can occur because the earth is both elastic and plastic.

Forces at its surface change the crust of the earth. Wind, water, and glaciers erode the face of the earth. They wear down mountains and tear away the soil. In this chapter and the next, we shall learn how the crust of the earth can also be changed by forces inside the earth. The changes due to these internal causes are often far greater than those caused by erosion. Earthquakes, volcanoes, and mountains are all due to pressures inside the earth,

Diastrophism

The change in the earth's crust due to these internal pressures is called *diastrophism*. The crust may be stretched, or reshaped, or it may even be snapped apart. Heat and pressure can cause a surge of hot liquid rock to the surface of the earth. A great earthquake can shatter the crust of the earth for hundreds of miles. Hundreds of square miles of the crust can be shoved high into the air. All of these changes in the crust are examples of diastrophism. When the change is very great, it is usually permanent. Such great changes are not frequent. This is fortunate for us, since the really great changes in the surface of the earth cause immense damage to life and property. Small changes, caused by stretching of the crust, go on at all times. We do not notice them because they do not cause any effects we can see.

Causes of Diastrophism

Nothing can change in our universe without the use of energy. Where does the energy come from? Changes in the earth's crust use energy from three sources: *first*, the heat from the inside of the earth; *second*, the pressure on the crust from heavy weights like mountains or piles of sediment; *third*, the pressures caused by the rotation of the earth. The amount of energy that can be supplied by these sources is really amazing. A volcanic explosion can throw millions of tons of earth far into the atmosphere. A large earthquake uses more energy than could be produced by a thousand hydrogen bombs.

Heat Inside the Earth

If we dig into the crust of the earth, we find that the temperature rises steadily as we go below the surface. The change in temperature is not the same in all parts of the world. In some mines the temperature is only 150°F far below the surface. But in parts of the United States, the temperature rises several hundred degrees at a depth of a few hundred feet. The average change all over the earth is 1°F for every sixty feet we go below the surface. The temperature of a three-hundred-foot mine is about 5° warmer at the bottom than on the surface.

Why does the earth grow warmer inside? We do not really know the answer to this question. Many scientists believe that the earth is still cooling off from its original hot condition. But new facts show that the earth may really be growing warmer and not colder. The extra heat may come from radioactivity inside the earth. We do not really know at this time which theory is correct. We do know that the earth is very hot inside the crust. At the bottom of the crust, about thirty-five miles down, the temperature is close to 1,000°C.

The high temperatures inside the earth melt some of the rock to liquid form. This liquid is under great pressure. If the pressure becomes too great, the melted rock can open a hole in the crust and force its way to the surface. We must remember that the earth is spinning very rapidly on its axis. This spinning can put great pressure on the crust. When we think of the weight that the crust must hold, like a large mountain, and add the heat and the pressure on the crust due to rotation and heat, we can see that the crust is really under a great strain all the time. It is not surprising that it cracks, or breaks, under these forces.

Earthquakes

When these pressures cause the crust of the earth to shift or crack, an *earthquake* may occur. There are many earthquakes each year but most of them are too small to cause damage on the surface. A large earthquake can tear an entire city apart in a few minutes. The break in the crust may be a crack or split. Or we may find a large block of crust raised above the rest. Whatever the shape of the break, it is always called a *fault*. The figure below shows a typical fault.

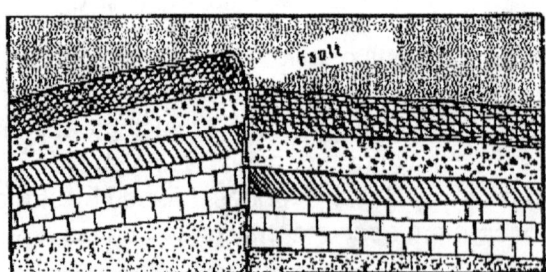

Vertical Fault in Earth's Crust.

One section of crust has raised up above the other. You can see the layers of rock that have been broken. The fault pictured here is called a vertical fault because one part of the crust rose above the other. The crust can also slide apart and make a horizontal fault. The break separates the two parts of the crust. Sometimes, the shift of the crust is twenty or thirty feet wide on the surface. These horizontal faults usually cause more damage then vertical faults.

To summarize, then, every year there are thousands of small faults in the crust of the earth. They occur on dry land as well as under the oceans. Most of the faults are small and can be recorded only with special equipment. The earth is under a constant strain. It gives a little here and a little there to make adjustments, just as our bodies do. As you walk your bones are under a steady strain. You do not notice the strain unless it becomes too great and a bone breaks to relieve the pressure. This is like an earthquake inside the body. The earth handles small strains easily. But once in a while the pressures build up, and a really serious break takes place.

Fortunately, we do not have many serious earthquakes. They can be devastating. The great earthquake in Lisbon in 1755 lasted only five minutes, but it ruined half the city and killed thousands of people. Thousands more were drowned when a great tidal wave hit the city after the earthquake. In 1906, when a bad earthquake struck California, the city of San Francisco was ruined. The crust shifted more than twenty feet in some places. Buildings collapsed, pipes were torn apart, and the whole city went up in flames. An earthquake in 1923 destroyed almost all of the city of Tokyo and also the city of Yokohama. These earthquakes were lateral quakes. The earth shifted horizontally, that is from side to side. An earthquake that lifts part of the surface does not cause such great damage. An earthquake in 1989 interrupted the landscapes in the San Francisco - Oakland Bay area. Earthquakes may produce large tidal waves - up to a hundred feet high - that do additional damage to areas struck by the earthquake as well as other areas.

The Earthquake Belts

Some parts of the world are not bothered with earthquakes. In other places the people live in constant fear of a major eruption. There are, in fact, two large earthquake "belts" that form loops around the Middle East and the Pacific Ocean. One includes northern Africa, the Alps Mountains, and southwestern Asia. Burma lies in this area. It has many violent earthquakes. But the worst earthquake region lies around the shores of the Pacific Ocean. The western coast of North and South America and the eastern coast of Asia suffer great earthquakes. The coast of Asia produces some really bad ones. Smaller tremors seem to take place a dozen times each day in places like Japan. These two belts have more than 90 percent of all the earthquakes in the world. We know the location of the two loops, but we still do not know exactly why the earthquakes occur.

The people who live in earthquake regions can take some precautions against disaster. They can avoid building towns or cities beneath large hills or bluffs. This eliminates the danger of the large cave-in that might drop masses of rock into the city. Houses can be built of material that will bend with the earthquake. Brick and stone should not be used for houses unless a steel frame is also used. Earthquakes cannot be prevented, but danger of loss of life and property can be lessened by careful management.

Making Mountains

When the earth was first cooled enough to form a crust, it was probably flat and smooth. Since that time, the forces inside the earth have produced the tremendous mountain ranges that we now see. Different kinds of mountains are made by different processes. But all of them have been raised by the energy inside the earth.

When hot liquid rock, or *lava,* is thrown out of the earth, it cools and forms a solid mass. A layer of cooled lava builds up around the hole in the earth. As this happens over and over again, the pile of lava grows. Whole mountains have been built by this process. Mount Shasta in northern California is a volcanic mountain of this type. The mountains in Hawaii were also produced by hot lava flowing from inside the earth. A volcanic mountain usually produces a cone-shaped peak.

A second type of mountain is made by the carving away of loose material, leaving the mountain of rock standing upright. These mountains are called *residual* mountains because the mountain is what remains after erosion takes place. The Catskill Mountains in New York were formed this way.

When a great block of the earth's crust is shoved high into the air, another type of mountain is formed. The block of crust can be hundreds of miles wide, and it may be pushed two or three miles into the air. The Sierra Nevada Range in California was built this way. The range is four hundred miles long and about one hundred miles wide. The whole mass of crust was thrust several thousand feet into the air.

Fold Mountains

Most of the great mountain ranges in the world were built by still another process. If you place a piece of cloth on a table, and push the ends together, the cloth forms a set of wrinkles in the middle. Now if you raise the whole mass of wrinkles into the air, you have a complete mountain range. This process is called folding, and it is the way really large mountain ranges are formed. Of course, it is not so easy to form wrinkles in a layer of rock eight miles thick as in a piece of cloth. Try to imagine enough energy to fold together hundreds of miles of crust, several miles thick, then shove the whole wrinkled crust up into the air. All of the energy we produce on earth could not do this job. But the force inside the earth is so great that it can do it. Given time, it will produce mountains like the Alps.

A folded mountain is produced by a three-step process. First, a great weight, such as a pile of sediment, causes the crust of the earth to sag and stretch. Second, the crust around the sagging area then presses in toward the gap. This creates huge wrinkles in the crust. Third, the whole mass of wrinkles is forced high into the air by pressures from below the surface, to form the mountain range. This process takes thousands of years. It has produced the Alps Mountains in Europe, the Andes Mountains in South America, and the Rocky Mountains in the United States and Canada.

These mountain chains are thousands of miles long, hundreds of miles across, and two or three miles high. The folding process thrusts the entire mountain area far above the surface of the crust. In fact, there has been enough energy inside the earth to shove the mountains upward two or three times. Geologists have learned that the Rocky Mountains and Andes Mountains have been lifted higher into the air at least three times in the past.

Earthquakes and mountains are the result of movements in the crust of the earth. In the next chapter we shall study a third type of activity in the earth's crust - the flow of hot liquid rock. This is called volcanic activity. Of course, both mountain making and earthquakes probably require great supplies of heat energy. Volcanic actions give us a better illustration of the movement of liquid rock. All three types of activity are a reminder that our earth is far from dead and buried. Inside the crust, tremendous amounts of energy are stored. When they break loose in the form of an earthquake, or a volcano, or a mountain, man is completely helpless. All we can hope to do is to keep the damage to a minimum. Perhaps we may be able to control these forces better when we learn exactly how they work. That is what scientists hope. That is one of the reasons why we spend much of our time trying to learn how and why changes in the earth's crust take place.

CHAPTER VII. VOLCANOES

You learned that the heat inside the earth produces great pools of liquid rock. Because the pools are beneath tons of rock, the liquid is often under great pressure. When a hole appears in the crust of the earth, the liquid rock pushes up through the hole to the surface. This flowing of hot liquid rock to the surface of the earth is part of what we call *volcanic activity*. Volcanic action can produce large mountains by building up layers of hard rock. Volcanoes also are closely related to earthquakes.

The melted rock inside the earth is called *magma*. When the melted rock comes to the surface, it is usually called *lava*. When magma hardens, it forms igneous rock. Magma is a mixture of melted rock, steam, and gases. The steam and gases create the great pressure that causes the volcano to explode. Of course, many volcanoes do not explode. They allow the magma to flow out of the earth in an even stream. This reduces the pressure inside the earth and prevents an explosion. Volcanic action includes both the explosions and steady flow of magma to the surface.

The Origin of Volcanoes

How do volcanoes begin? We do not really know, since we cannot look inside the earth to see. But geologists do know that there is very hot material below the surface of the earth. They believe that this is responsible for most volcanic action. Since many volcanoes are found near mountains that have recently been formed, some scientists believe that the great weight of the mountains plays some part in volcanic action. Perhaps the pressure caused by the mountain causes the flow of magma to the surface. No matter how a volcano begins, we know that great heat and pressure are needed to produce the energy which volcanic action employs.

Types of Volcanic Action

We usually think of a volcano as a great cone spouting flame and fire and rock. But, as we have said, many volcanoes do not explode at all. Volcanoes that ooze hot lava without exploding are more common. When the liquid rock moves out of the earth, the pressure inside is reduced, and consequently the danger of explosion is also reduced. Of course, the hot liquid rock is of itself quite dangerous. But it usually moves slowly, and so there is time for people to move away from it.

There are many types of volcanic activity. The speed of the action and the size of the explosion depend upon the type of magma and the amount of pressure behind the volcano. If magma is thick and viscous, it will not flow easily. Gas pressure has time to build up behind it. Therefore, an explosion is more likely to occur when the magma is thick. If the magma is thin, it flows easily and quickly. It can move out of the earth before there is time for the pressure to build up energy enough for an explosion. The actual viscosity of magma depends upon the type and temperature of the rock. Usually, hot magma is thinner and it flows more easily than cool magma.

The amount of gas trapped inside the earth also plays an important part in volcanic action. If there is little or no gas or steam, the volcano will not build up much pressure. It will probably not explode. But when a great deal of gas and steam is trapped in the volcano, an explosion is likely to occur. A volcanic explosion is like one big puff from a steam engine. The steam and gas is released from the engine by the puff; the hot magma is blown out of the earth by the explosion.

A Volcano in Action

What do we find when we look under the surface to see how a volcano works? All volcanoes begin with a great pool of liquid rock, or magma. The hot magma may melt more rock, increasing the size of the pool. When the magma touches a pocket of water, it turns the water to steam. Since water expands about 1,700 times when it changes to steam, this produces enormous pressure on the magma pool. Other gases inside the earth add to the pressure. If the pool of magma is trapped under the earth's crust, the pressure will force the magma toward the surface. If the crust is thin and weak, the pool of magma can cause a large hump in the earth. The pressure may make a crack in the crust, allowing the magma to flow out onto the surface of the earth. If the crust is strong and heavy and the magma under very great pressure, an explosion can take place, bursting through the crust. Then we have a really large volcanic explosion.

Some of these pools of magma exist beneath the floor of the ocean. When the crust breaks, the mixture of the hot lava with water produces enormous clouds of steam. Great clouds of steam are produced by the contact of the hot magma with the water.

Volcanic Explosions

You can imagine what will happen if a large pool of magma, trapped under solid rock crust, finally builds up enough pressure to explode. Some of the most terrific explosions on earth have been due to volcanoes of this type. In 1815 a volcano in the Dutch East Indies (now Indonesia) blew forty cubic miles of material into the air. This would fill a pit two miles wide, two miles deep, and ten miles long. Some of the rocks were thrown twenty miles into the air. The whole earth was covered with ashes from the explosion. Tidal waves more than a hundred feet high were created by the blast. Thousands of persons were killed by the explosion, which was heard for several hundred miles. Thousands more drowned in the giant tidal waves. A thousand miles away, the sky was so dark that lights were needed. This was the greatest volcanic explosion ever recorded.

Volcanic Craters

When a volcanic explosion occurs, it blows an enormous hole in the crust of the earth. An explosion in Alaska opened a hole two miles wide and over three thousand feet deep, for example. These holes in the crust are called volcanic *craters*. Sometimes, a new cone will build up inside the crater left by an old volcano. Mount Vesuvius in Italy, for example, is located inside the crater caused by the explosion of another Mount Vesuvius nearly two thousand years ago. When a volcano is quiet for many years, wind and water erosion cuts away the sides of the crater.

When the center has collapsed, we call the pit a *caldera*. Cal-deras are often very beautiful. The inside of the crater fills with water. The cliffs rise straight into the air from the water's edge. Many calderas are world famous beauty spots. In Hawaii, for example, the craters of two great volcanoes have formed calderas containing lakes nearly three miles wide. The cliffs above the lakes are several thousand feet high. They rise almost straight into the air above the water.

Lava Flow

Volcanic action also includes the flow of lava through a crack in the earth's crust. This type of action is not as spectacular as a great explosion. But it can make great changes on the face of the earth. Enormous areas have been covered by liquid rock from volcanoes. In India alone, nearly 200,000 square miles of land is covered with cold lava. Some parts of the layer are over two thousand feet thick. In the northwestern part of the United States, an even larger area is covered with volcanic lava. The layer is only five hundred feet thick, but it covers almost a quarter-million square miles of surface. Of course, this flow of lava took place thousands of years ago. But we are trying to see how the crust of the earth has been changed by volcanic action. And thousands of years is not a long time in terms of the life of the earth.

Active Volcanoes

Many of the volcanoes on earth are still active. They are very dangerous to life and property, and they cannot be controlled. But we can often get an advance warning when a volcano is about to explode. Before an explosion can take place, pressure must build up inside the earth. This pressure may cause small earthquakes to occur. Cracks may appear in the volcano, and hot lava may flow out through the cracks. These signs may indicate a coming explosion. Of course, there are areas in which earthquakes occur almost every day, and no explosion follows. But a large number of small quakes is often a sign of a coming explosion.

Probably as we learn more about the way heat circulates inside the earth, we may be able to predict volcanic action better. At present we are not really certain why volcanoes erupt. We need more scientific knowledge in this area before we can control the actions of nature that cause the trouble or take steps to protect ourselves against disaster.

Other Volcanic Action

Many types of volcanic action take place entirely below the surface of the earth. We do not see the effect on the surface. The hot magma inside the earth can move from place to place because of the pressure behind it. When it finds an opening, magma flows through the opening wherever it may lead. For example, magma often flows in between the layers of the earth. This causes an effect like a blister on the finger. These blisters are filled with liquid magma. They can produce a dome-shaped swelling on the earth if they are near the surface.

When magma finds a crack in the earth, it fills it just as a plasterer fills a crack in the wall. These filled cracks are called *dikes* if they are vertical. If they are horizontal, they are called *sills*. Some of the dikes are several miles wide and hundreds of miles long. The magma may also be forced into larger zones in the earth's crust and may fill them full of liquid rock. The great pressure behind the magma acts like a grease gun in a garage. It forces magma into other rocks. When the magma cools, it forms a solid plug of rock in the earth's crust.

Hot Springs and Geysers

The hot interior of the earth heats any water trapped deep in the crust. When this hot water flows to the surface of the earth through a crack, we have a *hot spring*. The hot water dissolves many of the minerals in the rock, and hot springs are usually filled with mineral water. In Europe and in the United States, these hot springs are used as health baths. Many people believe that it is healing to bathe in the hot mineral water.

If the hot water from inside the earth is thrown out in a great jet, we have a *geyser*. The western part of the United States has many of these geysers in action. A geyser comes from a crack in the earth that fills with water. At lower levels pressure builds up inside the crack as the water is heated. When the pressure is high enough, it throws the water into the air. Then the geyser stops flowing and begins to build up pressure once again. Some geysers erupt every few minutes. Others may take several days before they raise the pressure high enough to erupt. A geyser is like a volcanic pool that is filled with water. When the pressure reaches the trigger point, the water is driven into the air, and the pressure is relieved.

Using Volcanic Power

Can we harness the tremendous energy supply locked in the earth and put it to work? The use of volcanic power is like the use of the power of the tides. It can be used, but it is more expensive than the use of coal or petroleum. Volcanic energy is used to a limited extent in some areas. Some houses in Iceland are heated by hot water from the interior of the earth. Steam generated by hot magma is also used to produce electricity. But there are many problems involved. The steam from a volcano contains acids that eat into metals. This makes it hard to use with ordinary equipment.

The problem of location is also a difficult one. A volcano in Indonesia is of no use to the people of the United States and not much use to the people of Indonesia. If the volcanoes were located near large industrial centers, some use might be made of them. Some of the acids in volcanic gases are being recovered and sold. This, however, is only a small business at the present time. Until our supply of coal and petroleum becomes much smaller, or until we discover some simple way of using volcanic power, we will probably allow the power inside the earth to go untapped.

———

270 BASIC PRINCIPLES OF PHYSICS, CHEMISTRY, AND GEOLOGY

CONTENTS

Page

PRINCIPLES OF PHYSICS   1
   I.   General Properties of Energy and Matter   1
   II.   Mechanics of Solids   1
   III. Mechanics of Liquids   2
   IV.   Mechanics of Gases   2
   V.   Heat   3
   VI.   Sound   4
   VII. Light   5
   VIII. Magnetism   6
   IX.   Static Electricity   5
   X.   Current Electricity   6
   XI.   Atomic Energy and Radiation   6

PRINCIPLES OF CHEMISTRY   8
   I.   Chemical Nature of Water   8
   II.   Structure of Matter   9
   III. Solutions and Colloids   10
   IV.   Ions in Solution-Electrolytes   10
   V.   Carbon and Organic Chemistry   11

PRINCIPLES OF GEOLOGY   12
   I.   Diastrophism and Vulcanism   12
   II.   Degradation

270 BASIC PRINCIPLES OF PHYSICS, CHEMISTRY AND GEOLOGY

I. GENERAL PROPERTIES OF ENERGY AND MATTER

1. Energy can be changed from one form to another, or to matter, with exact equivalence.
2. Fluids have no elastic limit for compression.
3. The distortion of an elastic body is proportional to the force applied provided the elastic limit is not exceeded.
4. All liquids are compressible but only to a slight degree.
5. Gases may be converted into liquid by reducing the speed of their molecules.
6. If the vapor pressure of the water of hydration is greater than that of the moisture of the air, crystals will gradually yield up water to the air, and vice versa.
7. The free surface of a liquid contracts to the smallest possible area due to surface tension.
8. A liquid will rise in a capillary tube if the contact angle between the liquid and the side of the tube is less than 90° and will be depressed if the contact angle is greater than 90°.
9. The height to which a liquid rises in a capillary tube is directly proportional to the surface tension of the liquid and inversely proportional to the density of the liquid and to the radius of the tube.

II. MECHANICS OF SOLIDS

10. When forces act in the same direction, the resultant is their algebraic sum.
11. When two forces act upon the same object, the resultant is the diagonal of a parallelogram whose sides represent the direction and magnitude of the two forces. A single force represented by the diagonal may be resolved into two forces represented by the sides of the parallelogram.
12. When the resultant of all the forces acting on a body is zero, the body will stay at rest if at rest, or it will keep in uniform motion in a straight line if it is in motion.
13. A spinning body offers resistance to any force which changes the direction of the axis about which the body rotates.
14. Any two bodies attract one another with a force which is directly proportional to the attracting masses and inversely proportional to the square of the distance between their centers of mass.
15. Movements of all bodies in the solar system are due to gravitational attraction and inertia.
16. The period of a pendulum swinging through short arcs is independent of the weight of the bob but varies directly as the square root of the length and inversely as the square root of the acceleration of gravity.
17. The speed gained by a body with constant acceleration is equal to the product of the acceleration and the time.
18. The acceleration of a body is proportional to the resultant force acting on that body and is in the direction of that force.
19. The distance a body travels, starting from rest with a constant acceleration, is one-half the acceleration times the square of the time.
20. At any point on the earth's surface all bodies fall with a constant acceleration which is independent of the mass or size of the body if air resistance be neglected.
21. The amount of momentum possessed by an object is proportional to its mass and to its velocity.

22. When one body exerts a force on a second body, the second body exerts an equal and opposite force on the first.
23. Bodies in rotation tend to fly out in a straight line which is tangent to the arc of rotation.
24. Centrifugal force is directly proportional to the square of the velocity, to the mass, and inversely proportional to the radius of rotation.
25. The energy which a body possesses on account of its motion is called kinetic energy and is proportional to its mass and the square of its velocity.
26. The energy which a body possesses on account of its position or form is called potential energy and is measured by the work that was done in order to bring it into the specified condition.
27. The work obtained from a simple machine is always equal to the work put into it less the work expended in overcoming friction.
28. When there is a gain in mechanical advantage by using a simple machine, there is a loss in speed and vice versa.
29. In the lever, the force times its distance from the fulcrum equals the weight times its distance from the fulcrum.
30. In the inclined plane, weight times height equals acting force times length, providing friction is neglected and the force is parallel to the plane.
31. Sliding friction is dependent upon the nature and condition of the rubbing surfaces, proportional to the force pressing the surfaces together, and independent of area of contact.
32. The amount of heat developed in doing work against friction is proportional to the amount of work thus expended.

III. MECHANICS OF LIQUIDS

33. Any homogeneous body of liquid free to take its own position will seek a position in which all exposed surfaces lie on the same horizontal plane.
34. The pressure in a fluid in the open is equal to the weight of the fluid above a unit area including the point at which the pressure is taken; it therefore varies as the depth and average density of the fluid.
35. The pressure at a point in any fluid is the same in all directions.
36. When pressure is applied to any area of a liquid in a closed container, it is transmitted in exactly the same intensity to every area of the container in contact with the liquid.
37. As the velocity of flow through a constricted area increases, the pressure diminishes.
38. A body immersed or floating in a fluid is buoyed up by a force equal to the weight of the fluid displaced.
39. The rate of osmosis is directly proportional to the difference in concentration on opposite sides of the membrane.

IV. MECHANICS OF GASES

40. The atmospheric pressure decreases as the altitude increases.
41. The atmospheric pressure decreases with increasing water vapor content, other things being equal.
42. A fluid has a tendency to move from a region of higher pressure to one of lower pressure; the greater the difference, the faster the movement.
43. In the northern hemisphere great volumes of air revolve in a counterclockwise direction, and in the southern hemisphere, they revolve in a clockwise direction.
44. In moving air, wind pressure increases as the square of the velocity.

45. The volume of an ideal gas varies inversely with the pressure upon it, providing the temperature remains constant.
46. If the same pressure is maintained, the volume of a gas is varied directly as the absolute temperature.
47. If the volume of a confined body of gas is kept constant, the pressure is proportional to the absolute temperature.
48. When a mixture of gases is confined, each exerts its own pressure without reference to the pressure exerted by others.
49. Diffusible substances tend to scatter from the point of greatest concentration until all points are at equal concentration.
50. A gas always tends to expand throughout the whole space available.
51. The speed of diffusion of gases varies inversely with the square root of their densities.

V. HEAT

52. The average speed of molecules increases with the temperature and pressure.
53. Most bodies expand on heating and contract on cooling; the amount of change depending upon the change in temperature.
54. The total change in length of a metal bar is equal to its coefficient of linear expansion times the original length times the change of temperature in degrees Centigrade.
55. A change in state of a substance from gas to liquid, liquid to solid, or vice versa, is usually accompanied by a change in volume.
56. Substances which expand upon solidifying have their melting points lowered by pressure; those which contract upon solidifying have their melting points raised by pressure.
57. Heat is liberated when a gas is compressed, and is absorbed when a gas expands.
58. Heat is conducted by the transfer of kinetic energy from molecule to molecule.
59. When two bodies of different temperature are in contact, there is a continuous transference of heat energy, the rate of which is directly proportional to the difference of temperature.
60. Heat is transferred by convection, in currents of gases or liquids, the rate of transfer decreasing with an increase in the viscosity of the circulating fluid.
61. The principal cause of wind and weather changes is the unequal heating of different portions of the earth's surface by the sun; thus all winds are convection currents caused by unequal heating of different portions of the earth's atmosphere, and they blow from places of high atmospheric pressure to places of low atmospheric pressure.
62. Radiant energy travels in waves along straight lines, its intensity at any distance from a point source is inversely proportional to the square of the distance from the source.
63. The more nearly vertical the rays of radiant energy, the greater the number that will fall upon a given horizontal area, and the greater is the amount of energy that will be received by that area.
64. The lower the temperature of a body, the less the amount of energy it radiates; the higher the temperature, the greater is the amount of energy radiated.
65. Dark, rough, or unpolished surfaces absorb or radiate energy more effectively than light, smooth, or polished surfaces.
66. Bodies of land heat up and cool off more rapidly and more readily than bodies of water.
67. The atmosphere of the earth tends to prevent the heat of the earth's surface from escaping, and the earth begins to cool only when the amount of heat lost during the night exceeds that gained during the day.

68. Solids are liquefied and liquids are vaporized by heat; the amount of heat used in this process, for a given mass and a given substance, is specific and equals that given off in the reverse process.

69. The amount of heat which a constant mass of liquid or solid acquires when its temperature rises a given amount is identical with the amount it gives off when its temperature falls by that amount.

70. Every pure liquid has its own specific boiling and freezing point.

71. The presence of a dissolved substance will cause the resulting solution to boil at a higher temperature and to freeze at a lower temperature than pure water.

72. Freezing point depression and boiling point elevation are proportional to the concentration of the solution.

73. The boiling point of any solution becomes lower as the pressure is decreased and higher as the pressure is increased.

74. The rate of evaporation of a liquid varies with temperature, area of exposed surface, and saturation and circulation of the gas in contact with the liquid.

75. The rate of vaporization decreases with an increase of concentration of the vapor in the gas in contact with the liquid, the temperature remaining constant.

76. Condensation will occur when a vapor is at its saturation point if centers of condensation are available and if heat is withdrawn.

77. When a gas expands, heat energy is converted into mechanical energy.

78. The higher the temperature of the air, the greater the amount of moisture required to saturate it.

79. The pressure of a saturated vapor is constant at a given temperature, and increases with an increase of temperature.

80. Each combustible substance has a kindling temperature which varies with its condition, but may be greater or less than the kindling temperature of some other substance.

VI. SOUND

81. Sound is produced by vibrating matter and is transmitted by matter.

82. When energy is transmitted in waves, the medium which transmits the wave motion does not move along with the wave, but the energy does.

83. Each vibrating particle in a wave front of any wave motion may be considered as a secondary source of spherical wavelets which spread out from their sources with the velocity of the primary wave.

84. The velocity of sound is directly proportional to the square root of the elasticity modulus and inversely proportional to the square root of the density of the transmitting medium.

85. The speed of sound increases with an increase in temperature of the medium conducting it.

86. The velocity of a wave is equal to the product of its frequency and wave length.

87. Sound waves are reflected in a direction such that the angle of incidence is equal to the angle of reflection.

88. Musical tones are produced when a vibrating body sends out regular vibrations to the ear while only noises are produced when the vibrating body sends out irregular vibrations to the ear.

89. The loudness of a sound depends upon the energy of the sound waves and, if propagated in all directions, decreases inversely as the square of the distance from the source.

90. The higher the pitch of a note, the more rapid the vibrations of the producing body.

91. When a sounding body is moving toward or away from an observer the apparent pitch will be higher or lower, respectively, than the true pitch of the sound emitted.
92. The frequency of the vibration of a stretched string is inversely proportional to its length, diameter, and square root of its density; and directly proportional to the square root of the stretching force.
93. The quality of a musical tone is determined by the pitch and intensity of the different simple tones or harmonics into which it may be resolved.
94. Harmonious musical intervals correspond to very simple frequency ratios.
95. Two sound waves of the same or nearly the same frequency will destructively interfere with each other when the condensations of the one coincide with the rarefactions of the other provided that the directions of propagation are the same.
96. Sound waves or other energy impulses may set up vibrations in a body the amplitude of which is increased if the impulses are exactly timed to correspond to any one of the natural periods of vibration of the body.

VII. LIGHT

97. Energy is often transmitted in the form of waves.
98. Waves travel in straight lines while passing through a homogeneous or uniform medium.
99. When waves-strike an object, they may be absorbed, transmitted, or reflected.
100. Whenever an opaque object intercepts radiant energy traveling in a particular direction, a shadow is cast behind the object.
101. Light travels in straight lines in a medium of uniform optical density.
102. The speed of light in any given substance bears a constant ratio to the speed of light in air.
103. The intensity of illumination decreases as the square of distance from a point source.
104. When light rays are absorbed, some of the light energy is transformed into heat energy.
105. The darker the color of a surface, the better it absorbs light.
106. If a beam of light falls upon an irregular surface, the rays of light are scattered in all directions.
107. When light is reflected, the angle of incidence is equal to the angle of reflection.
108. All rays passing through the center of curvature of a mirror are reflected upon themselves.
109. In a plane mirror a line running from any point on the object to the image of that point is perpendicular to the mirror.
110. An image appears to be as far back of a plane mirror as the object is in front of the mirror and is reversed.
111. When light is incident upon a medium in which it will travel faster and when the angle of incidence is greater than the critical angle, it is totally reflected.
112. When parallel light strikes a concave spherical mirror, the rays, after reflection, pass directly through the principal focus only if the area of the mirror is small compared to its radius of curvature.
113. When light rays pass obliquely from a rare to a more dense medium, they are bent or refracted toward the normal and when they pass obliquely from a dense to a rarer medium, they are bent away from the normal.
114. The dispersion of white light into a spectrum by a prism is caused by unequal refraction of the different wave lengths of light.
115. Parallel light rays may be converged or focused by convex lenses or concave mirrors, diverged by concave lenses or convex mirrors.

116. The curvature of a wave front will be changed a given amount by a lens; namely, 1/F.
117. The sum of the reciprocals of the conjugate focal lengths of a lens or mirror equals the reciprocal or the principal focal length.
118. The dimensions of an image produced by a lens or a mirror are to the dimensions of the object as their respective distances from the lens or mirror are to each other.
119. The colors of objects depend upon what light rays they transmit, absorb, or reflect.
120. Incandescent solids and liquids emit all wave lengths of light and give a continuous spectrum.
121. When white light passes through a substance that absorbs some waves and not others, certain bands of color are missing with the production of an absorption spectrum.
122. Luminous vapors and gases emit only certain kinds of light producing bright-line spectra.
123. When a body which emits a bright line spectrum is moving toward or away from the observer, the lines are shifted toward the short or long wave length end of the spectrum, respectively.
124. A beam of light may become plane polarized as the result of any circumstance which results in the suppression of one of the rectilinear components of the vibration without affecting the components at right angles to it .

VIII. MAGNETISM

125. Pieces of iron, steel, cobalt, or nickel may become magnetized by induction when placed within a magnetic field.
126. A magnet always has two poles and is surrounded by a field of force.
127. Like magnetic poles always repel each other and unlike magnetic poles always attract each other.
128. The force of attraction or repulsion between two magnetic poles varies directly as the product of the pole strengths and inversely as the square of the distance between the poles.
129. Magnets depend for their properties upon the arrangement of the metallic ions of which they are made up.

IX. STATIC ELECTRICITY

130. Electrons have both a magnetic and an electric field.
131. Like electrical charges repel and unlike electrical charges attract.
132. In an uncharged body there are as many protons as electrons and the charges neutralize each other; while a deficiency of electrons produces a plus charge on a body and an excess of electrons produces a negative charge.
133. The force of attraction or repulsion between two small charged bodies varies directly as the product of the two charges and inversely as the square of the distance between the charges.
134. Electrostatic induction is the separation of charges on a conductor through the influence of a neighboring charge.
135. Charges on a conductor tend to stay on the surface and to be greatest on the sharp edges and points

X. CURRENT ELECTRICITY

136. An electric current may be produced in four ways: by rubbing or friction, by chemical action, by the use of magnets, and by induction.
137. An electric current will be produced in a closed circuit including two strips of different metals if one of the junctions is heated or cooled.

138. An electric current will flow in the external circuit when two metals of unlike chemical activity are acted upon by a conducting solution, the more active metal being charged negatively.

139. Electrons will always flow from one point to another along a conductor if this transfer releases energy.

140. Gases conduct electric currents only when ionized.

141. Electrical power is directly proportional to the product of the potential difference and the current.

142. The electrical current flowing in a conductor is directly proportional to the potential difference and inversely proportional to the resistance.

143. All materials offer some resistance to the flow of electric current, and that part of the electrical energy used in overcoming this resistance is transformed into heat energy.

144. The resistance of a metallic conductor depends on the kind of material from which the conductor is made, varies directly with the length, inversely with the cross-sectional area, and increases as the temperature increases.

145. In a parallel circuit the total current is the sum of the separate currents, the voltage loss is the same for each branch, and the total resistance is less than the resistance of any one branch.

146. In a series circuit the current is the same in all parts, the resistance of the whole is the sum of the resistance of the parts, and the voltage loss of the whole is the sum of the voltage losses of the parts.

147. An electrical charge in motion produces a magnetic field about the conductor, its direction being tangential to any circle drawn about the conductor in a plane perpendicular to it.

148. When a current-carrying wire is placed in a magnetic field, there is a force acting on the wire tending to push it at right angles to the direction of the lines of force between the magnetic poles, providing the wire is not parallel to the field.

149. In a transformer the ratio between voltages in the primary and secondary circuits is the same as that between the number of turns of wire in these circuits.

150. Positively charged ions of metals may be deposited on the cathode, as atoms, when a direct current is sent through an electrolyte.

151. The mass of any substance set free by electrolysis is proportional to the current flowing and the time of flow; if the quantity of electricity is kept constant the masses of the various substances set free are proportional to their electrochemical equivalents.

152. The amount of heat produced by an electric current is proportional to the resistance, the square of the current and the time of flow.

153. Energy in kilowatt hours is equal to the product of amperes, volts and time (in hours), divided by one thousand.

154. An e. m. f. is induced in a circuit whenever there is a change in the number of lines of magnetic force passing through the circuit.

155. An induced current always has such a direction that its magnetic field tends to oppose the motion by which the current was produced.

156. The magnitude of an induced e. m. f. is proportional to the rate at which the number of lines of magnetic force change and to the number of turns of wire in the coil.

157. Two electro-magnetic waves having the same frequency and amplitude and traveling in normally the same direction will interfere constructively or destructively, depending upon whether they are in phase or out of phase.

158. Electro-magnetic waves may produce electrical oscillation in a condenser circuit which is so adjusted as to oscillate naturally with the same frequency as that of the incoming waves.

159. Condenser capacitance varies directly with the area of the plates and inversely as the thickness of the insulation between them.

160. Alternating current charges a condenser twice during each cycle inducing opposite charges on the two plates with the result that a current appears to flow through the condenser.
161. By means of high frequency generators or vacuum-tube oscillators, sustained or continuous oscillations can be produced in a condenser circuit. Their intensity is made to vary with audio-frequency currents in a transmitter circuit to produce radio waves.
162. Whenever a high-frequency oscillating current produces in the field around it oscillating electric and magnetic fields, energy in the form of an electromagnetic wave is transmitted through space.

XI. ATOMIC ENERGY AND RADIATION

163. In a tube which contains gas at low pressure subject to an intense electric field, cathode rays, streams of electrons, move away from the negatively charged terminal at high speeds.
164. A number of substances will emit electrons and become positively charged when illuminated by light.
165. Electrons are emitted from any sufficiently hot body.
166. Electrons change energy levels emitting or absorbing energy.
167. When a stream of high speed electrons strikes a body, the atoms of that body emit X-rays.
168. The atoms of all radioactive elements are constantly disintegrating by giving off various rays (alpha, beta, and gamma) and forming helium and other elements.
169. Radioactive emission involves nuclear changes.
170. Radioactivity is independent of all physical conditions: heat; cold, pressure, and chemical state.
171. Matter may be transformed into energy and energy into matter; the sum total, matter plus energy, remains constant.
172. Elements may be changed into other elements.
173. Atoms have great subatomic energy.
174. All matter is made up of protons, neutrons, and electrons.
175. Protons and neutrons only are found in the nucleus of an atom.
176. Some elements have more than one atomic weight due to differences in the neutron content of their nuclei.
177. The mass of an atom is concentrated almost entirely in the nucleus.
178. The distances of successive electron shells from the nucleus of an atom and from each other are much greater than the dimensions of the nucleus itself.
179. Atoms may be broken down by bombarding the nucleus with high speed particles such as protons, alpha particles, and neutrons.
180. Atoms or molecules may lose electrons when struck by high speed electrons or ions.

PRINCIPLES OF CHEMISTRY

I. CHEMICAL NATURE OF WATER

181. Every pure sample of any substance, whether simple or compound, under the same conditions will show the same physical properties and the same chemical behavior.
182. A pure chemical substance may be prepared from raw materials through utilization of their physical and chemical properties.
183. Each element has its own characteristic X-ray spectrum.

184. Every chemical element when heated to incandescence in a gaseous state has a characteristic glow and a characteristic spectrum which can be used to identify very small quantities of the element and which is related to the molecular and atomic structure of the gas.

185. In every sample of any compound substance formed, the proportion by weight of the constituent elements is always the same as long as the isotopic compositions of each element is constant.

186. When different amounts of one element are found in combination with a fixed weight of another element (in a series of compounds), the different weights of the first element are related to each other by ratios which may be expressed by small whole numbers.

187. At a definite temperature and pressure, the relative combining volumes of gases and of gaseous products may be expressed approximately in small whole numbers.

188. The materials forming one or more substances, without ceasing to exist, may be changed into one or more new and measurably different substances.

189. The products of reacting substances may react with each other to form the original substances.

190. The total mass of a quantity of matter is not altered by any chemical changes occurring among the materials composing it.

191. No chemical change occurs without an accompanying energy change.

192. The heat of formation of any chemical compound equals its heat of decomposition.

193. When a chemical change takes place without the addition of heat from an external source, that substance which has the greatest heat of formation will tend to form.

194. Reactions occurring at ordinary temperatures are predominately exothermic.

II. STRUCTURE OF MATTER

195. All matter is composed of single elements or combinations of several elements and can be analyzed by chemical processes and divided into these constituents.

196. All substances are made up of small particles called molecules, which are alike in the same substance (except for variations in molecular weight due to isotopes) but different in different substances.

197. Elements are made up of small particles of matter called atoms which are alike in the same element (except for occasional differences in atomic weight, i.e., isotopes) but different in different elements.

198. The orderly arrangement of molecules, atoms, or ions in crystals gives crystals regular form.

199. Equal volumes of all gases under similar conditions of temperature and pressure contain very nearly the same number of molecules.

200. Atoms of all elements are made up of protons, neutrons, and electrons; and differences between atoms of different elements are due to the number of protons and neutrons in the nucleus and to the configuration of electrons surrounding the nucleus.

201. The electrons within an atom form shells about the nucleus, each of which contains a definite number of electrons.

202. Most atoms have the property of losing, gaining, or sharing a number of outer shell electrons.

203. The properties of the elements show periodic variations with their atomic numbers.

204. The energy shown by atoms in completing their outer shell by adding, losing, or sharing electrons determines their chemical activity.

205. The valence of an atom is determined by the number of electrons it gains, loses, or shares in chemical reactions.

206. A few elements are inert or chemically inactive because their atoms are so constructed as to be complete in themselves; i. e., their outer electron rings have no tendency to gain or lose electrons.

207. The gravimetric composition of a compound may be found by multiplying the atomic weights of the elements by their subscripts in the formula of the compound.

208. Equal amounts of heat raise equal numbers of atoms of all elements in the solid state through nearly equal intervals of temperature.

209. The specific heats of many elements are approximately inversely proportional to their atomic weights.

210. Oxidation always involves the removal or sharing of electrons from the element oxidized, while the reduction always adds or shares with the element reduced.

211. Oxidation and reduction occur simultaneously and are quantitatively equal.

212. Metals comprise a group of elements (other than hydrogen) whose atoms have a tendency to lose electrons readily and whose compounds when dissolved in polar solvents are capable of forming positive ions.

213. Non-metals comprise a group of elements whose atoms tend to gain or share electrons and whose compounds, when dissolved in polar solvents, are capable of forming negative ions.

214. Metals may be arranged in an activity series according to their tendency to pass into ionic form by losing electrons.

215. Non-metals may be arranged in an activity series according to their tendency to pass into ionic form by gaining electrons.

III. SOLUTIONS AND COLLOIDS

216. The ingredients of a solution are homogeneously distributed through each other.

217. Any substance soluble in two immiscible liquids will distribute itself between the two in proportion to its solubility in the two liquids.

218. The solubility of solutes is affected by heat, pressure, and the nature of the solute and solvent.

219. The solubility of a gas in an inert solvent varies directly with the pressure to which a gas is subjected.

220. In a saturated solution, the product of the molar concentrations of the ions is constant.

221. Suspended particles of colloids have a continuous, erratic movement due to colloidal, molecular, or ion impacts.

222. Surface reactions predominate in all non-homogeneous reactions.

223. Colloids show greater chemical activity than the solid substances in mass, since rates of reaction are proportional to the surface area of the solid, other factors being equal.

224. Colloids have the property of absorption to an unusual degree.

225. Colloidal particles may carry electrical charges.

226. Temperature changes, pressure changes, the presence of electrolytes or the presence of oppositely charged particles may cause colloids to precipitate.

IV. IONS IN SOLUTION - ELECTROLYTES

227. All chemical reactions which start with the same quantities of original substances, liberate the same amounts of energy in reaching a given final state, irrespective of the process by which the final state is reached.

228. If stress is applied to a reversible chemical system, there will be a readjustment in the system to relieve the stress.

229. The speed of chemical reaction is increased by increasing the concentration of any of the reactants; and is decreased by decreasing the concentration of any of the reactants.
230. Chemical reactions may be carried more nearly to completion by any condition that establishes an unusually low concentration of one of the products.
231. Whenever the product of the concentrations of any two ions in a mixture exceeds the value of the ion-product in a saturated solution of the compound formed by their union, this compound will be precipitated.
232. Whenever the product of the concentrations of any two ions in a mixture is less than the value of the ion-product in a saturated solution of the compound formed by their union, this compound, if present in the solid form, will be dissolved.
233. Simple ionic reactions are typically rapid reactions.
234. The rates of many reactions are affected by the presence of substances which do not enter into the completed chemical reaction.

235. Acids and bases are substances which in water solution ionize to give hydrogen and hydroxyl ions, respectively, from their constituent elements.
236. The activity of an acid or base is proportional to the degree of ionization of the compound when in solution.
237. The exchange of the negative and positive ions of acids and bases results in the formation of water and a salt.
238. Salts of strong acids and strong bases undergo negligible hydrolysis, while salts of inactive acids and inactive bases undergo more marked hydrolysis.
239. Electrolytes dissolved in water exist partially or completely as electrically charged particles called ions.
240. The properties of alloys are dependent upon the relative amounts of their components, the extent of their compound formation,8 and upon the crystalline structure of the mixture.

V. CARBON AND ORGANIC CHEMISTRY

241. Carbon atoms form a number of "type groups" of compounds which are determined by the elements present and by the structural combinations of the atoms within the molecules.
242. Unsaturated hydrocarbons are active chemically and form many compounds by addition.
243. Saturated hydrocarbons are relatively inactive chemically but form compounds by substitution.
244. The boiling point of hydrocarbons increases with an increase in molecular weight.
245. Molecules of some compounds undergo polymerization.
246. Alcohols react with acids to form esters and ethers.
247. Alcohols oxidize to aldehydes, ketones, and acids.
248. Elements and compounds to which the cells of living organisms react specifically produce physiological effects.
249. The enzymes, vitamins, and hormones are chemical regulators of the reactions that occur in living organisms.

PRINCIPLES OF GEOLOGY

I. DIASTROPHISM AND VULCANISM

250. The earth's surface may be elevated or lowered by interior forces.
251. Forces within the earth may cause breaks to appear in the earth's crust.
252. Under the high pressures which occur in the earth's interior, materials that usually are solid have the capacity to flow slowly and thus bring about equalization of pressure differences on the surface.
253. Earthquakes are produced by the sudden slipping of earth materials along faults.
254. Rocks may be folded to form mountains.
255. Strata of rooks occur in the earth's crust in the order in which they were deposited, except in the case of over thrust faults..
256. Igneous rock may be formed from materials intruded into other rocks.
257. Rocks may be formed by the cooling and solidifying of molten material.
258. Rocks may be formed by the compacting and cementing of sediments.
259. Rocks may be metamorphosed, or changed, by heat, pressure, and flexion.

II. DEGRADATION

260. Parent material for the development of soils is formed through the physical disintegration and chemical decomposition of rock particles and organic matter.
261. The natural movements of air, water, and solids on the earth are due chiefly to gravity plus rotation of the earth.
262. When elevations or depressions are created upon the surface of the earth, the elevations are usually attacked by the agents of erosion, and the materials are carried to the depressions.
263. The rate of erosion is inversely proportional to the resistance of rocks to decomposition and disintegration.
264. Continual erosion results in decreasing the average density of continental masses, and continual deposition in increasing the average density of rocks under the ocean.
265. Streams, generally, are lowering the surface of land in some places and building it up in other places.
266. The transporting power of streams varies approximately as the fifth power of the velocity.
267. Streams, potentially, have a regular cycle: youth, maturity, and old age.
268. Falls or rapids tend to develop in a stream bed wherever the stream flows over a hard stratum to a soft one.
269. Glacial abrasion occurs in proportion to the weight of the ice and the velocity of its movement.
270. Glacial conditions are as a rule approached by increasing latitudes or altitudes.

———

CPSIA information can be obtained
at www.ICGtesting.com
Printed in the USA
BVHW010902140220
572397BV00014B/268